The Nautilus® Book

ELLINGTON DARDEN, Ph.D.

CONTEMPORARY
BOOKS

CHICAGO

Library of Congress Cataloging-in-Publication Data

Darden, Ellington, 1943–
   The Nautilus book / Ellington Darden.
      p.   cm.
   Bibliography: p.
   Includes index.
   ISBN 0-8092-4074-2 (pbk.)
   1. Nautilus weight training equipment.   2. Weight training.
I. Title.
GV548.N38D37   1988
796.4'1028—dc 19   88-423
                                                   CIP

Important Notice

Do not use, adjust, or operate Nautilus equipment without proper instruction by owner-authorized personnel.

Keep hands and feet away from weights and other moving parts while machine is in use. Never put hands or feet under weight stacks. Be sure to keep hands or feet located only on hand grips and foot pads provided.

Do not operate equipment with loose or damaged parts. Notify owner-authorized personnel of any problems with equipment.

Failure to comply with these instructions may result in personal injury.

Nautilus® is a registered trademark of Nautilus Sports/Medical Industries, Inc.

Published by Contemporary Books, Inc.
Two Prudential Plaza, Chicago, Illinois 60601-6790
Manufactured in the United States of America
International Standard Book Number: 0-8092-4074-2

Other Books of Interest
by Ellington Darden, Ph.D.

For a free catalog of Dr. Darden's books, please send a self-addressed, stamped envelope to Nautilus Sports/Medical Industries, PO Box 160, Independence, VA 24348.

Contents

Preface

In 1990 Nautilus introduced a full line of commercial exercise machines to the fitness industry. These new machines, called Next Generation, are improved versions of one of the world's most recognized products.

This edition of *The Nautilus Book* features the Next Generation machines. It also shows many of the older machines for those who still use them. Whether the Nautilus machines you use are old, new, or in between, this manual will direct you in getting maximum results from your training.

In addition to how-to photographs and instructions for the Nautilus machines, you'll get an updated philosophy of what Nautilus is and is not. Much of the research for the philosophy section was done by Ken Hutchins, who worked for Nautilus for over ten years. Ken resides in Orlando, Florida, where he continues to uncover new insights into proper exercise.

The Next Generation photographs of Holly Pellham, Jerry

Coronado, and Blake Boyd are by Dan Howard. Other photographs are by Chris Lund and Tim Tew.

The Nautilus Book is the most comprehensive guide ever written on the Nautilus way to fitness. Use it to your advantage!

Ellington Darden, Ph.D.

Dr. Ellington Darden has been director of research for Nautilus Sports/Medical Industries since 1973.

Terri Jones demonstrates the women's pullover machine.

I.
The Nautilus Philosophy

Every Nautilus machine incorporates scientifically designed cams
and sprockets that correctly vary the resistance according to your
potential strength curve.

This provocative poster was produced by Parker Turner
of Shreveport, Louisiana.

1
Nautilus Emerges

In 1970, after 20 years of experimentation, Arthur Jones built and sold an exercise machine. It was a pullover machine for the torso muscles. This was the first tool on the market to provide variable, balanced resistance. The resistance was varied and balanced by the use of carefully designed eccentric cams, or spiral pulleys.

As Jones was studying the spiral pulleys, it occurred to him that they resembled a section of the chambered nautilus shell. The chambered nautilus is a mollusk that, because of its geometric perfection, has survived at the bottom of the Pacific Ocean for millions of years. It was an ideal symbol for the new machines. A year later the new company in Lake Helen, Florida, became Nautilus Sports/Medical Industries. Since then Nautilus exercise machines have revolutionized the concept of training and conditioning the human body.

The reason Nautilus revolutionized physical conditioning

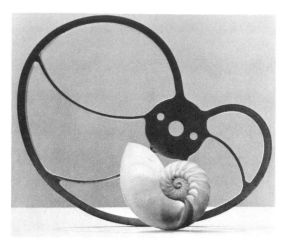

Arthur Jones's original spiral cams reminded him of a section of a chambered nautilus shell; so he named his new exercise machines Nautilus.

was, in one word, efficiency. Nautilus training was much more efficient than traditional methods of exercise. Earlier methods of conditioning had centered around long programs of exercise. To obtain a high level of fitness, an individual had to spend a minimum of 90 minutes a day on stretching for flexibility, jogging for heart-lung endurance, and lifting barbells for strength. The average fitness enthusiast might spend from 5 to 10 hours a week on such exercise programs.

If Nautilus machines required the same amount of time as traditional methods and produced slightly better results, that would still be a worthwhile contribution. But producing three times the results in only a fraction of the time could only be described as revolutionary. And that is exactly what Nautilus produced: three times the results in a fraction of the time!

Nautilus machines first gained publicity in the bodybuilding field. After being trained by Arthur Jones and his machines for six months, 19-year-old Casey Viator won the 1971 Mr. America contest with obvious ease. Not only did he win the main title, but he took all the awards for body parts with the exception of best abdominals. He remains the youngest man ever to win the title. His victory in the Mr. America contest attracted the attention of football coaches to Nautilus strength-building machines. Soon Nautilus was being used for football conditioning. In 1972 the Miami Dolphins were the first National Football League team to incorporate Nautilus into their conditioning program. The Cincinnati Bengals followed suit, as did the Houston Oilers and the Buffalo Bills. Now 27 of the 28 teams use the equipment.

The Washington Redskins, winners of the Super Bowl in 1988, have one of the finest Nautilus off-season and in-season programs in professional sports. Much of their success can be attributed to their strength-training coach, Dan Riley. Riley came to Washington in 1982 after establishing a highly productive Nautilus program at Penn State University.

The National Football League's use of Nautilus machines gave considerable credibility to their effectiveness. Now teams in other sports such as basketball, hockey, baseball, wrestling, and swimming also employ Nautilus in their training programs.

This interest naturally aroused the attention of the fitness and health centers catering to millions of nonathletes across

The first Nautilus machine displayed to the public was at the 1970 Mr. America contest in Culver City, California. The machine was 15 feet long, 6 feet wide, 8 feet high, and had four stations: pullover, behind neck, rowing, and pulldown. (Photo by Inge Cook)

the nation. As Nautilus effectiveness was demonstrated, more and more fitness centers began ordering full sets of Nautilus equipment. Nautilus fitness centers began to spring up in all major cities. By the end of 1990 there were more than 9,000 fitness centers using Nautilus equipment.

Nautilus machines are also used by sportsmedicine clinics, hospitals, rehabilitation centers, law enforcement agencies, the armed forces, government agencies, YMCAs, professional sports teams, colleges, high schools, corporate recreation centers, exercise physiology laboratories, racquetball and tennis clubs, and individuals. Sales are both national and international.

In 1986 a new transition took place at Nautilus Sports/ Medical Industries. Arthur Jones, weary of the day-to-day business side of the company, sold Nautilus to Ward International of Dallas, Texas.

Four years later Ward International sold the company to a group headed by Dan Baldwin, former president of Nautilus and chief of manufacturing for twelve years. Baldwin moved the corporate headquarters from Dallas to Independence, Virginia, where the majority of manufacturing is done.

In the 1990s Nautilus will continue to produce commercial exercise machines and expand into new areas, such as home machines, multistation equipment, and diet programs. Each of these categories will be discussed later in this book.

Gaining access to Nautilus machines is merely the intitial step in obtaining superior results from exercise. Using Nautilus equipment correctly is of equal importance. Function dictates design, and each Nautilus machine is designed according to the physiological functions of the human body. An understanding and application of the guidelines presented in this book will allow you to obtain the best possible results from Nautilus training.

2
The Confusion of Exercise and Recreation

Nautilus equipment provides the ultimate form of exercise—very productive but intensely demanding.

Nautilus exercise is *not* recreation. It should not be construed as fun.

Many people confuse exercise with recreation. To obtain maximum results from Nautilus, it is important that you clearly understand the differences between exercise and recreation.

EXERCISE DEFINED

In exercise, the body performs work of a demanding nature. The key word here is *demanding*. The work is so demanding that the body's physical and metabolic status quo is threatened, though not really harmed. An alarm is sounded: "Body, your protective margins are inadequate. Adapt to these imposed demands or you will not survive!" Improved physical fitness then occurs over the next several days.

The general principle of exercise is *intensity*. Its subprinciples are duration, frequency, form, selection of movement, and progression.

High-intensity exercise is unpleasant to perform. Great motivation is required to reach momentary failure in an exercise when muscles ache, the lungs burn, and nausea becomes a real possibility. These uncomfortable feelings are reminding us that we are imposing demands on our bodies that make the worthwhile improvements possible.

Five physical benefits can be derived from proper exercise:

1. increased muscular size, strength, and endurance
2. enhanced joint flexibility
3. improved heart-lung efficiency
4. increased body leanness
5. reduced risk of musculoskeletal as well as cardiovascular trauma, this benefit being a result of the first four

In a more general sense, exercise does only three things—and two of the three are bad.

First, exercise stimulates your body to become stronger. After this stimulation, and in order for the overcompensation process to occur, your body requires adequate rest, nutrition, and, most important, *time.*

Second, exercise beyond the minimum amount for stimulation prevents optimum results. It uses up your body's valuable recovery ability.

Third, exercise, if done improperly, produces injury. All the worthwhile results from exercise are produced by your body. It adapts, it grows, it improves. Exercise does not produce these gains. It merely stimulates your body to produce them. So injury remains the only direct result of exercise. This should be a sobering commentary to the overenthusiastic fitness buff.

RECREATION ACKNOWLEDGED

Another measure of general fitness is mental health. Psychological well-being is manifested in many forms, and most psychologists agree that recreation and fun are healthy aspects of our daily lives. Fun activities are important and personal. You may not enjoy the same activities as do your neighbors. Perhaps that is why there are so many different leisure-time diversions.

Sports and many vocations are equally recreational for different persons. This may explain, in part, where a very fundamental problem often arises.

Reflect for a minute on the exercise history of our ancestors. Is it not likely that running as exercise developed concurrently with the need to run to catch prey and to avoid becoming prey? Is it not likely that competition developed to hone survival skills? Is it not likely that swimming as sport, exercise, and a need to propel the body through water developed simultaneously? Notice the same interrelationship in wrestling, shot-putting, pole-vaulting, gymnastics, and most of the activities we now call sports. This leads to several wrong conclusions: that recreation constitutes exercise, that exercise should be fun, and that any movement or activity constitutes exercise.

This bears repeating: what is recreational for you may not be for someone else. Your choice of recreational activities is personal, but the fact that it provides pleasure and amusement is the most important determining factor in making that choice.

In addition to personal choice, you should answer some other questions before undertaking a chosen form of recreation:

1. Are you aware of the dangers involved in this form of recreation?
2. Are you willing to accept the dangers?
3. Are you willing to prepare to protect yourself from those dangers?

A man crippled from a game of tackle football—undertaken by his own choice—has no grounds to complain. If he expects to play such a brutal game in total safety and to ignore the dangers and preparation, then he has no business on the gridiron.

SHARP DIFFERENCES

Contrary to popular belief, exercise and recreation are polar in many ways. They represent exact opposites in substance, as illustrated below:

Exercise	*Recreation*
Logical	Instinctive
Universal	Personal
General	Specific
Physical	Mental
Not Fun	Fun

Let's look at these sharp differences one at a time.

Exercise Is Logical, Recreation Instinctive

Exercise is a logical strategy designed around the body's muscular functions. No attempt should be made to simulate in exercise what takes place in a sport. Exercise is, therefore, clinically controlled.

Recreation is instinctive. It represents an activity that we

Brenda Hutchins trains this middle-aged woman on basically the same Nautilus exercises as she would train a woman trying to make the Olympic team. (Photo by Ken Hutchins)

would prefer to do. It is governed and directed by our personal whims.

In bodybuilding there is a philosophy known as the *instinctive training theory*. The proponents of this idea suggest that the best approach to exercise is to follow your instincts. In other words, if you feel like training today, then do so. If you feel a layoff is appropriate, then it is. If you feel like performing a set of situps at the beginning of your workout instead of at the end, then "listen to your body."

Arthur Jones laid this concept to rest in many minds when he wrote, "If you followed your instincts, you would do quite a number of things—eat as much as possible, sleep whenever convenient, fornicate, lie, brag, steal, run away from danger, and avoid any form of physical labor. But you wouldn't exercise [paraphrased]." So much for the instinctive training theory.

Exercise Is the Same for Everybody

Exercise is universal; recreation is personal. There are no distinctive exercise regimens special to pregnant women, rehabilitation, osteoporotics, or football linebackers. Exercise is designed for human beings. The principles of exercise, the muscular structures and functions, and the biology are the same in every case. Granted, there are some precautions that pregnant women or patients in rehabilitative therapy may have to take. But the *general* approach to exercise is the same for everybody.

Specificity in Exercise—A Great Fable

Better skill in an activity should improve the efficiency of that movement. But skill training is a realm of its own, separate and distinct from exercise performed for physical enhancement. Skill training is specific to the activity practiced. Exercise is general.

Some writers in the area of sports and fitness apply the term *specificity* to physical conditioning. There is no such principle in exercise. Specificity is the exclusive principle of motor-learning science. Exercise should result in general and overall physical improvements that contribute to *any* skill, sport, vocation, or recreation. For the most part, exercise is not specific.

Exercise for the Body, Recreation for the Mind

Exercise is physical. Through exercise we are attempting to stimulate physical improvements in the body. Yes, physical improvement should and does lead to psychological improvement in most cases. But a better self-concept and outlook on life are the aftereffects of proper exercise, not the instantaneous rewards.

Many motivational aspects of exercise are indeed personal. Goal setting and possibly educational perspectives are individualized factors in any exercise program. Also, a great deal of

Performed properly, the Nautilus multi-triceps machine provides demanding overload to the upper arms.

mental concentration is required to learn and to execute controlled and isolated muscular movements. Such motivation, again, depends on the subject's awareness that his reward will follow his physical performance.

Recreation, on the other hand, is not consciously performed for the sake of any reward beyond itself. It is performed because it brings about a pleasurable and satisfying feeling.

Exercise Is Not Fun

Remember, if you exercise properly, you place demands on your body. These demands are manifested in labored breathing, increased pulse, raised blood pressure, increased metabolic rate, and several other temporary phenomena. Experiencing such changes is far from pleasant for most people. And motivating any training subject is difficult. Exercise is simply unpleasant, hard work.

The logical application of exercise pits intellect against instinct. This results in an uncomfortable internal tension.

Recreation should be fun. Fun is not the only characteristic or requirement of recreation, but it is the most important. This is not to say that some aspects of a person's chosen pastime do not carry some aspects of toil. Americans, by and large, go to a lot of trouble to have fun. They often lug their families and many of their personal belongings to vacation and picnic areas to relax and enjoy themselves with all the comforts of home. This is a humorous paradox often portrayed in cartoons produced by the Disney Studios.

A COMMON COURSE OF EVENTS

The fundamental result of the recreation and exercise confusion is that many people perceive their vocations or pastimes as exercise.

Typically, a businessman completes his yearly physical examination with his physician. His physician recommends that he select a leisure activity to relieve his mounting stress. Exercise is also recommended but is not distinguished from recreation.

The businessman may choose tennis. The result: since tennis is rarely intense, the exercise effect is grossly compromised. If tennis is mistaken for exercise, the fun aspect suffers.

The ideal approach to any form of recreation is this:

First, give an affirmative answer to the questions posed earlier for choosing a form of recreation.

Second, condition yourself physically, not through the recreational activity but through high-intensity Nautilus exercise. Accept Nautilus exercise for what it is—*hard work.* Do not attempt to enjoy it other than by collecting a certain amount of satisfaction and confidence that you are showing steady physical improvements. Attempt to become adequately flexible and lean and as strong, enduring, and resistant to injury as possible.

Then play tennis or engage in whatever pastime you have chosen. You can play your game better, practice better, learn its skills more quickly, and enjoy it more completely. You will also be more resistant to injury. This is recreation and exercise as they should be combined.

3

The Present State of Fitness

Addressing the Florida Physical Education Association's annual convention in Orlando, Arthur Jones immediately got the audience's attention when he stated:

"If everyone in the United States realistically rated his or her lifetime average physical fitness on a scale from –10 to 10, the combined overall average would be –4. Physical fitness activities have caused more harm than good. Furthermore, if everyone in the United States suddenly stopped participating in fitness activities, the health of the nation would improve significantly within a matter of weeks. The average score would soon rise closer to 0."

Although the above is an opinion, medical statistics do reveal that every year 20 million Americans suffer injuries that require medical consultation due to fitness, recreational, and sports activities. That figure, if interpreted as casualties, is costing the United States more yearly in terms of broken bodies than the combined total sustained in all of our wars since

1776. And those consequences generally are produced *in the pursuit of health*!

James Michener, in his book *Sports in America*, commented that if so many injuries and fatalities were produced by some dread disease such as polio or tuberculosis or were the result of some criminal element, the American public would band together. We would sponsor telethons, raise funds, and deliver speeches to denounce and stamp out the villain. But sports and recreational activities? They're OK.

"For most of our citizens," wrote Jerry Kirshenbaum and Robert Sullivan in the February 7, 1983, issue of *Sports Illustrated*, "the heralded physical fitness boom is a bust." Much of the fitness business, they say, is a hard-sell hustle. Madison Avenue copywriters and authors of magazine cover stories have been breathlessly proclaiming the reality of such a boom for more than five years. Naturally, such hype is to their benefit.

"To say that the U.S. is caught up in a fitness boom," continued Kirshenbaum and Sullivan, "is to imply that Americans have become fitter, and while there are plenty of people around who swear that this is the case, the evidence strongly suggests otherwise. There's reason to believe that whatever wonders the fitness boom may have worked for certain individuals, it hasn't made society as a whole fitter at all."

All of the above writers would argue that exercise has enormous potential benefit *when* it is applied sanely. But so far, few Americans are getting those benefits. Exercise can and should lead to an improved quality of life. Just the opposite prevails in most cases.

There *are* serious problems with the current physical fitness situation in the United States. Many of the problems, once again, are based on a failure to distinguish between exercise and recreation.

CONTINUUM OF RECREATION

Imagine a broad continuum of possible activities for recreation. At one end might be those such as knitting, chess, stamp collecting, building model airplanes, and billiards. These activities impart little or no exercise effect to the body. An emotional game of Monopoly might stir the heart, but to label it exercise would stretch the meaning to the meaningless.

On the opposite end of the continuum are activities of a more athletic nature. Still performed primarily for the purpose of fun are sports such as tennis, jogging, racquetball, basketball, hockey, baseball, weightlifting, swimming, dancing, and many more done in the name of exercise. But they are really not exercise. They are merely recreational activities that coincidentally impart some exercise effect—a slight and incomplete effect at best.

Exercise may be a reason for performing some of the more athletic forms of recreation. But in this instance exercise almost always takes a remote backseat to many unacknowledged psychological and sociological priorities.

For the sake of analysis, let's examine the following three forms of recreation: jogging, yoga, and weightlifting. How do they measure up in providing all five of the definite physical benefits—muscular strength, joint flexibility, heart-lung endurance, body leanness, and fewer injuries?

AN ANALYSIS OF JOGGING

In *Sports in America*, which was published in 1976, an orthopedic surgeon for the New York Jets football team, Dr. James Nicholas, noted that the probability of incurring an injury serious enough to require medical consultation from playing tackle football for just a year was 86 percent. So what? Most people know that football on any level of competition is a traumatic activity.

About the same time, *Runner's World*, a magazine with a vested bias in favor of running, published an article reporting a similar incidence of injury for jogging: 80 percent. And since football medical records are much more complete as compared to the records for jogging enthusiasts who may sprain their knees or suffer similar injuries but refuse to see a doctor, 80 percent is no doubt a conservative figure.

After hearing those statistics, an orthopedic physician who had jogged enthusiastically for several years smiled and replied, "The figure for jogging injuries is wrong. Try 100 percent!" This is certainly a slight exaggeration for emphasis, but it demonstrated what he had learned from his experience. Connective tissue traumas resulting from jogging programs are as follows: stress fracture, shinsplints, ruptured vertebral disc, chondromalacia of the patella, ankle sprain, and knee sprain. And this list of injuries includes only some of the many impairments that can ensue from repetitive jogging.

Recent reports show that the incidence of stress fracture of the pelvis is markedly higher for women joggers than for men. This is particularly evident in women over age 30. Pelvic stress fracture often requires months of immobilization.

Benefits of Jogging

Jogging or running can raise one's pulse significantly, which usually leads to an improvement in the cardiovascular system. But this improvement is minimal compared to the improvements made possible by involving large muscle masses in high-intensity exercise.

What will jogging do to improve flexibility? Nothing. In fact, unless a separate flexibility program is performed simultaneously, the short-range movements in jogging lead to flexibility reductions.

What about muscular strengthening? Running of any kind represents overload to the otherwise inactive person, and some slight muscular hypertrophy and strengthening does take place. But this occurs for only the first few exposures to the increased activity. In fact, strength declines in joggers who are already stronger than average.

In regard to body leanness, and contrary to much publicized lay and medical opinion, movement activities burn few calories. Histologists tell us that fat tissue is the most efficient form of energy storage known to biology. One pound provides enough energy for the typical adult male to run nonstop for 35–45 miles. Alone, exercise is not an efficient method for losing fat.

Some rare individuals possess inefficient metabolisms and sustain quicker than average fat losses on running regimens, but most of the loss usually reported is weight, not fat.

Exercise remains essential to a fat reduction program but for reasons often unsuspected. Without the stimulus for muscle hypertrophy or at least maintenance, a moderately reduced caloric consumption results in *indiscriminate* tissue loss. Muscle, fat, and other tissue is lost. General wasting occurs that is not healthy.

If the caloric reduction is severe and in the absence of exercise, muscle and other vital tissues are lost at an alarming rate. Fat is preserved. Though weight is reduced, the percentage of body fat is increased. The health issue here is fat loss, and *scales cannot measure fat.*

Proper exercise induces *discriminate* reduction of fat with a safe, moderate dietary reduction. It also serves to burn more calories indirectly. Scientists say that the most expensive tissues to support calorically in the body are those of the nervous system and the muscles.

Nervous tissue cannot be increased, but muscle tissue can exhibit dramatic volume and strength changes. The possession of more muscle effectively raises metabolism at work and at rest. This can contribute significantly to the calories you can eat and remain lean or become even leaner. It is estimate that basal metabolism increases by 50–100 calories per day for each pound of muscle added to the average healthy adult.

Basal metabolism is the energy necessary to keep the body warm and alive during total inactivity. Approximately 70 percent of the average person's caloric expenditure is for basal metabolism. The remaining 30 percent is the energy used in all physical activity and digestion.

Since running-type recreations merely burn a few extra calories above that of normal daily activities, and muscular strengthening is not realistically induced, running and jogging contribute little to body leanness.

Does jogging increase resistance to injury? Increased resistance to injury should be an expected result of proper exercise. Added protection depends on several factors.

Efficient skill execution should lend to safer participation in recreational activities. Again, this is a matter of learning and practicing those exact skills. Jogging encourages skill improvement only in those activities that require jogging. There is little transfer to other specific skills.

Exercise should result in greater tissue integrity. Stronger muscles around the joints, stronger tendons and ligaments, and stronger bones are all the result of muscle hypertrophy, either directly or indirectly. Running programs do not promote tissue integrity. As already stated, just the opposite often occurs, and the injury rate is absurd.

Does Jogging Deserve a Place in Exercise?

This analysis is not meant to imply that running or jogging is bad. If you enjoy running *and* realize *and* accept *and* prepare for the dangers, then run! But do not call it exercise when applied this way. It may indeed be good recreation for those who enjoy the euphoria of a long run, the clearing of the mind, and the scenery of nature trails. But it's not for the typical American.

Running does, however, have one place as exercise. If a boot camp officer is ordered to train 500 new recruits into a semblance of physical condition in nine weeks, what practical choices are there?

Well, he can instruct them to perform a few group calisthenics and run. His options for exercise, efficient or poor, are extremely limited. He might consider partner-resisted exercises, but monitoring their performance would be impossible. The matched partners would simply pretend to resist one another with no real and worthwhile effort. What is left? To run them. Is it efficient? No, not for an individual, but it is the best possibility for a mass of 500.

YOGA EXAMINED

Yoga became quite popular during the 1960s and '70s. It is often noted for its benefits of mind control and relaxation through meditation as well as enhanced flexibility. Some practitioners demonstrate the remarkable ability to control their heart rate mentally.

Selected hatha yoga postures, done somewhat similar to calisthenics, can induce some exercise effect on the heart and lungs. This results because the movements are performed in a difficult manner.

Perhaps the most outstanding physical effect of yoga is extreme flexibility. This is shown by the bizarre positions sometimes assumed by its practitioners. The lotus position is one example.

Most children and adults, however, do not need increased flexibility. Many women, indeed, are hyperflexible as a by-product of their child-bearing ability. This hyperflexible, un-dermuscled condition of most women contributes signifi-cantly to the instability of their joints. They desperately need increased joint stability.

The supporting muscular strength about a joint is essential for its integrity. Stronger muscles possess better tonus and contribute greater stability at rest as well as during activity. And contrary to conventional belief, stronger muscles are generally more flexible muscles.

Flexibility is adverse when it becomes excessive with respect to the joints. Increased flexibility can cause injury! This is especially true in regard to stretched ligaments, evidenced by increased joint laxity.

Dr. Stanley Plagenhoef, of the University of Massachusetts, and Dr. Richard Dominguez, of Loyola University Medical Center, independently researched the documentation that suggests flexibility programs lend protection to athletes. Both researchers found that no studies ever concluded such a widespread belief. Admittedly, the idea sounds reasonable, and flexibility is an accepted requirement for fitness.

Note that the first mention of flexibility in this book as one of the five definite benefits of exercise listed it as "enhanced flexibility." It purposefully was not written "increased flexibility."

Drs. Plagenhoef and Dominguez agree that the importance of flexibility is currently overrated by sportsmedicine professionals. Going a step further, Dr. Plagenhoef proceeded to film a series of traumatic football injuries as they occurred. After analyzing the forces displayed in the films, he could make only one direct conclusion: the study failed to show that greater flexibility reduced or prevented any injury. Dr. Plagenhoef points out that this is not saying that flexibility might not lend greater protection to the athlete. His study simply failed to show any correlation.

Dr. Stanley Plagenhoef shows Ellington Darden some of the force and range of movement analyses that he has calculated with various athletes.

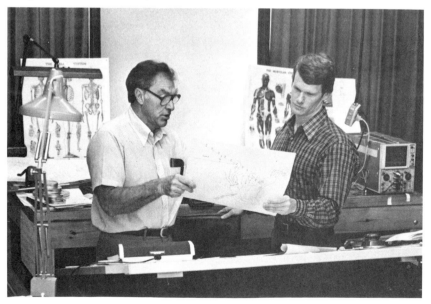

Dr. Plagenhoef also expressed two further conclusions based, not on the study, but on his experienced opinion. These opinions are common among informed sportsmedicine physicians:

- If the joints of an athlete, or anyone, are surrounded and supported by stronger muscles, then the chance of any trauma is reduced.
- If a joint in question becomes more flexible but without a corresponding increase in muscular strength, injury probability is *increased.*

The Importance of Flexibility

Please do not misunderstand the point of this discussion. Flexibility is important. The function of the joints is to bend, thereby permitting the muscles to produce movement. If the joints cannot bend, then movement is impossible.

Some activities, such as yoga, ballet, judo, karate, and gymnastics, require extreme flexibility, and a supplemental flexibility program may be suggested. But average men and women are not benefited by extreme flexibility. Just the opposite is likely.

Elderly people sometimes walk with a choppy gait because they have lost normal range of motion and muscular strength. The proper use of almost any exercise tool to increase their strength will simultaneously improve their flexibility. This occurs by virtue of the pressure applied during the negative portion of the exercise.

Yoga's Exercise Benefits

Apart from the misunderstanding concerning stretching, yoga can provide an exercise effect. It is mostly restricted to cardiovascular stimulation, however, and this depends largely on the movements performed and how they are performed. Again, considering the benefits of exercise, yoga is incomplete. There are far better methods for achieving cardiovascular improvement.

WEIGHTLIFTING AS A SPORT

The sport of weightlifting, which tests a person's maximum strength with a barbell, is a growing activity in America.

Weightlifting is considered one of the most dangerous sports. This is especially true in regard to the musculoskeletal system. Though perhaps not yet symptomatic, x-ray-detectable damage is present in almost 100 percent of participants who have competed for one year or more.

Weightlifting is actually misnamed. It should be called *weightthrowing*. In weightlifting competition the weights are hoisted vertically against gravity. But the technical skill required involves accelerating the mass vertically in such a manner that momentum allows the participant to *jump* under it.

The practice of competition lifts, such as the snatch and clean-and-jerk, enhances the skills the competing weightlifter must have. But developing these skills will do very little toward stimulating growth and thus strengthening the musculature. Other controlled, submaximal repetitions are performed that actually lend strength to the body.

As a result, weightlifters are markedly stronger than average people. They also suffer a host of injuries. Many of their training methods are certainly not efficient or safe for the purpose of acquiring muscular strength.

Contrary to popular belief, weightlifters are often more flexible in certain ranges of movement than the general population. This is due to a back pressure (force pulling in a direction opposite to the direction of movement produced by muscular contraction) provided in even the poorest application of the barbell. Weightlifters sometimes move about as though their flexibility is impaired, but this is usually an illusion created by the antics and unusual behavior they often effect. In some cases inflexibility *is* real, and this is most often

The snatch in competitive weightlifting involves bringing a barbell from the floor to a locked position overhead in one quick movement. Such weightlifting is very dangerous to the muscles and bones. (Photo by Bruce Klemens, courtesy *Iron Man* magazine)

the result of extreme overfatness among the superheavy-weight competitors.

Weightlifters seldom have above-average cardiovascular/pulmonary capacity. This is due to a defect not in the barbell but in how the training program is designed. Common practice dictates that weightlifters perform an exercise, wait several minutes, then perform another exercise or repeat the first. The rest period permits the heart rate to decline. To keep it elevated, rest must be restricted between exercises. The manner in which most weightlifters train, therefore, does not lead to increased cardiovascular fitness. This is not to say that it cannot or should not lead to improvements. In fact, the best possible cardiovascular benefits are possible from strength training, as we shall come to understand.

THE FITNESS CHALLENGE

Jogging, yoga, and weightlifting are commonly thought to offer valuable exercise to sports enthusiasts and fitness-minded people. All three activities serve to focus toward a different aspect of fitness. In each case the exercise effect can be small-to-medium at best or counter productive at worst. Most people would be better off finding something else to do with their exercise time. Please keep in mind that these comments do not include or address any possible recreational benefits. That is another matter altogether.

In the final analysis, your fitness challenge is as follows: Don't try to make exercise fun. Don't try to make recreation exercise. If you do, you grossly compromise the physical benefits of the exercise and the intended amusement of the recreation. Accept and apply both for what they are and the quality of your life will greatly improve.

4
The Evolution of Resistance

Pretend for a moment that you live in a vacuum where there is no influence of air, water, or gravity. There is no access to any mechanical device to impose resistance on your movements. Would you encounter resistance when you moved? Yes.

Muscles work in pairs. About the elbow joint are the muscles of flexion and extension. Contraction of the biceps muscle flexes or bends the elbow. Contraction of the triceps muscle extends or straightens the elbow. For the biceps to contract, the triceps must lengthen. The converse is also true.

In any exercise the muscle contracting against the resistance is termed the *agonist*; its opposing functional muscle is the *antagonist*. In a biceps curling exercise the biceps is the agonist, while the triceps is the antagonist.

The opposite is true in a triceps extension exercise. The triceps is agonistic, the biceps now antagonistic. The combined condition of the agonist-antagonist muscles is what some people refer to as *tonus*. Tonus is a term that in recent years has been commercially altered to *muscle tone*. But the correct word is still *tonus*.

Tonus refers to the residual tension in a muscle at rest. Generally, the stronger and larger the muscle, the greater the tonus. Tonus serves several important functions. It adds support about the joints at rest, keeps slack out of the muscle system, contributes to the body's shape, and supplements the body's protective barriers.

Some resistance is provided by the tonus of the antagonistic muscles as they are stretched during contraction of their complementary agonists. Such resistance is of poor quality and insufficient to provide adequate exercise for even maintaining the existing size and strength of the muscles.

As you might guess, the atrophy of muscles and loss of bone mass are real obstacles to prolonged projects performed in orbital weightlessness. This also explains why passive exercise is practically worthless except for rare rehabilitative applications.

But there is another possible source of resistance in the absence of weight. You could alternately extend and flex a particular body part with enough velocity to self-impose a momentum against which your muscles repeatedly accelerate and decelerate. Performed too quickly, however, even in a weightless environment, this would be dangerous to your body's structural integrity.

A significant improvement can be made with body movement against a weighted environment, however. The evolution of resistance stems from four different types of resistance: (1) dry-land/free-hand activities, (2) liquid-medium activities, (3) partner-resistance exercise, and (4) progressive exercise equipment.

DRY-LAND/FREE-HAND ACTIVITIES

Such activities as running, calisthenics, and dance would be

The push-up is a dry-land/free-hand activity that provides limited overload for the upper body. (Photo by Ellington Darden)

classified as *dry-land/free-hand activities* to distinguish them from those performed in liquid mediums and those performed with supplemental weight devices. All dry-land/free-hand activities are of about equal resistance quality. They can provide an overload only to muscles that have been relatively inactive. No progressive workload is realistically possible. Steeper grades or higher elevations are incorporated to impose greater demands on the body's systems. Exercise amount or speed can be increased, but the range of possible work levels is very narrow since the duration must be increased as well. Progression is not easily recorded, as performance monitoring is very subjective in these activities. High-intensity work cannot be maintained.

Dry-land/free-hand activities, therefore, do not offer an effective means of overload for the human body.

LIQUID MEDIUMS

Another possibility is performing continuous movement

against water. Since the gravitational effect on the body's mass is lessened by the buoyancy of water and water offers more limb resistance than air, swimming provides a wider range of work than dry-land/free-hand exercises. The work/duration provided by swimming, however, remains narrow. Yes, the speed and duration can be increased to provide more hydrostatic resistance, but greater limb speed can mean poorer muscle control, isolation, and, hence, intensity for individual structures.

Though liquid mediums offer improved resistance to the arms compared to air, they offer poorer resistance to the legs than the weight of the body against the earth on dry land. Still, muscular growth appears slightly better stimulated with water exercise than with dry-land/free-hand exercise. This may be due to the inherited characteristics of individuals who excel at swimming.

Dry-land/free-hand exercise has one distinct advantage over water activities. Swimming is almost devoid of negative work.

Positive work is common to most human movement. It occurs when a muscle contracts and shortens against resistance.

Negative work is performed as the muscle lengthens in a very controlled manner instead of entirely giving way to the imposed back pressure.

For example, lifting a brick with contraction of the arm muscles involves positive work. If you then drop the arm and the brick with no effort to slow its downward course, little negative work is performed. Controlled lowering takes place as a result of negative work.

For the purpose of increasing muscular strength, negative work appears superior to positive work. Controlled lowering involves better form and muscular isolation. Ensuring better form may be the primary factor behind the beneficial results of negative work.

Weight often provides a meaningful back pressure even in the poorest dry-land exercises. This back pressure includes at

Swimming provides
little
or no negative work for
the muscles.
(Photo by Inge Cook)

least the weight and torque of the torso and limbs against the muscles and bones. Negative work is almost totally absent in water. A small amount is provided by the buoyed body weight as well as the internal tonus of the muscles, but not by the water.

An indirect result of muscular growth is maintenance and/ or strengthening of the bones. Osteopenia, the loss of bone mass, occurs rapidly in a weightless environment. Buoyancy in water is likened to this weightlessness.

The apparently improved muscle growth in liquid mediums may compensate for its lack of meaningful negative work. But in the sense that fluids offer virtually no negative work, dry-land/free-hand exercise is superior to exercise done in a liquid.

Movements in a liquid medium do have practical applications as exercise. Here the limited progressive nature of fluids can be enhanced by increasing or decreasing their viscosities. Even then, it is still difficult to record accurately intensity and progression.

PARTNER-RESISTED EXERCISE

The first meaningful breakthrough in the application of high-intensity exercise was likely an accidental discovery. It came through wrestling, which has existed as sport, contest, combat, and exercise in many forms and in many customs throughout human history.

Wrestling is conscious movement against a somewhat-matched opponent. It often provides a significant intensity that can be sustained for only a few moments. When performed in a manner to avoid competition and to enlist complete stretch and contraction of major muscle groups, wrestling becomes partner-resisted exercise. It offers the possibility for very intense muscular work.

Partner-resisted movement provides a dynamic exercise effect when applied properly. This effect includes both muscular growth and stimulation of the heart and lung system. Partner-resisted movements still, however, do not satisfy all of

Wrestling is a form of partner-resisted exercise. (Photo by Inge Cook)

the requirements of high-intensity exercise, as you'll see in the next chapter.

Intensity must stay at a high level for exercise to remain beneficial. An overload must exist for continued adaptation. As the body adapts, the same workload is no longer registered as high intensity. Progressively greater workloads of briefer duration must be applied to maintain high intensity. Partner-resisted exercise is not practically progressive, because it also cannot be measured effectively.

PROGRESSIVE RESISTANCE EQUIPMENT

Stories of men who lifted growing animals abound in the historical and mythological literature. This was a rustic means of progressively overloading the musculoskeletal system. Also, stones, logs, and weighted vests are often described in training regimens of the past.

The major limitation of these latter devices was their nonprogressive nature. If a man was too weak to move a particular stone, he simply could not exercise with it. And if he could move that stone, he could progress only in the manner in which he lifted it. The manner in which it was lifted was meaningful, but its nonadjustable weight left much to be desired as far as being progressive or objective.

For exercise to be progressive, workloads must be at least crudely measurable. This became possible for the first time in 1902 with the invention of the plate-loading adjustable barbell.

"The adjustable barbell," Arthur Jones says, "is almost a miracle tool." This may seem unusual coming from the man who invented Nautilus equipment. But it's true. Before Nautilus machines were invented, the barbell was the foremost means of progressive exercise.

For a low cost, about $50 for a bar and 100 pounds of plates, almost every man and woman can own a barbell set and obtain physical improvements that can reward them for the rest of their lives.

When cost and productivity are added together
a barbell is an excellent buy.
(Photo by Ken Hutchins)

Properly applied, the barbell is capable of providing improvements in all five components of physical fitness. But the
barbell is almost never applied sanely or safely.

There are unavoidable problems with a barbell: namely, it
does not provide rotary resistance, balanced resistance, or
direct resistance.

Isometric, Isotonic, Isokinetic

The words *isometric, isotonic,* and *isokinetic* are commonly used to denote different methods of exercise. The intended meaning of these words, however, is different from their practical use.

The Greek prefix *iso* means same. *Metric* means measure. So *isometric* means same measure or same length. In isometric exercise the trainee supposedly contracts his muscle against an immovable object with the length of the muscle remaining the same. But this is not true. Some movement in the muscle does occur during isometric exercise.

Isotonic means same tonus. Since the tonus of the muscle has never been measured accurately, it is difficult to say whether this term can be applied to indicate what is really occurring in the muscle. Generally, *isotonic* has evolved to mean exercise that involves both positive and negative resistance.

Isokinetic, as used in exercise, suggests that the muscle contracts with a constant speed. *Kinesis* is the Greek root meaning motion. Some manufacturers prefer to say that their devices provide accommodating resistance—supposedly equal and opposite to the applied force. Regardless of the name or device, resistance is provided by some form of friction: mechanical or liquid. Because of the nature of isokinetic overload, there can be no negative resistance.

Isokinetic, isotonic, and *isometric* do not describe the internal muscular phenomenon for which they were invented. They more aptly describe the mechanics of the exercise device. *Isometric* involves little movement. *Isotonic* applies best to barbells, dumbbells, and conventional equipment. *Isokinetic* is based on friction and involves no negative resistance.

Generally Nautilus equipment is isotonic, but it's isotonic with some important additions, as you'll see in Chapter 5.

In the 1950s, several people started trying to improve the barbell. Machines such as the Universal Gym, which provided self-contained, pin-selector weight stacks, were introduced. It was no longer necessary to add or remove barbell plates. Instead resistance could be provided by moving a pin from one hole to another. Thus, the speed of use and the convenience were greatly improved. Perhaps most important, the machines offered exercise that was safer than barbell training. But an equal degree of results could still be produced by a barbell.

The problem with such machines was, and remains, the fact that they were simply copies of barbell exercises. Some people made the mistake of continuing to work within the limitations of a barbell. Instead, they should have been working within the limitations of human muscles.

One man did recognize this problem and did something about it. That man, of course, was Arthur Jones. In the process, Jones discovered the 10 requirements for full-range exercise. Full-range exercise is an important component in the evolution of resistance, and it will be discussed in detail in the next chapter.

5
Full-Range Exercise

Exercise must provide resistance and movement. The value of the exercise can be determined by the *quality of the resistance* and the *quantity of the movement.*

Arthur Jones recognized those facts in the 1930s, but it took him another 30 years to understand them completely, then define his thoughts, and finally build a working machine.

By 1948, however, Jones had made one major discovery—the importance of rotary resistance. The fundamental acknowledgment that human movement is rotary against a linear gravitational field was the first major step in the development of full-range exercise.

The 10 elements below are necessary for full-range exercise.

1. rotary resistance
2. positive work
3. negative work

4. stretching
5. prestretching
6. automatically variable resistance
7. balanced resistance
8. direct resistance
9. resistance in the position of full muscular contraction
10. unrestricted speed of movement

Once these needs are understood, it is possible to appraise the relative efficiency of any exercise tool. Let's examine each of the requirements.

ROTARY RESISTANCE

Muscular contraction occurs in an approximately straight line, and straight-line force is produced. But the body part that is moved by muscular contraction does not move in a straight line. Instead, the body part rotates, as it must, since it is working around the axis of a joint.

The articulation of the joints converts the straight-line force of muscular contraction into the rotary-form force required for movement. Much the same thing occurs in an engine when the crankshaft converts the straight-line power produced by the cylinders into the rotary-form power required by the wheels.

Most forms of exercise provide resistance in only one direction. This direction may be downward as a result of the force of gravity during barbell exercises. It may be upward (or across) during Universal Gym exercises, where the resistance is redirected by the use of pulleys or levers. Or it may be in any possible direction during isokinetic-type exercises. But in all three cases one facet remains constant: resistance is provided in only one straight-line direction.

Obviously, full-range exercise cannot coexist with straight-line resistance, since the body part involved is constantly changing its direction of movement through rotation. Resistance, therefore, is provided only at the start of an exercise movement, during the mid-range of movement, or at the end. It is not present throughout a movement.

Resistance is provided only when the direction of movement is opposed to the direction of the pull of the resistance. That is impossible when a person is trying to apply a straight-line source of resistance against a rotary-form movement. During a barbell curl, for instance, there is no resistance at all at the start of the movement. The resistance is pulling downward while the movement is forward. Thus the resistance is 90 degrees out of phase with the direction of movement.

Shortly after the curling movement is started the direction of movement changes to the point that the resistance is almost 90 degrees out of phase with the direction of movement. At this point some resistance is provided, but not much. That's because you're still pushing the weight more than you're lifting it.

Actually, you're lifting the weight only in one small area of movement, at the point where your hands are going straight up while the resistance is pulling straight down. This is the so-called *sticking point* of the curl, where the weight feels far heavier at that point than it is at any other point throughout the movement. But its direction of pull is exactly 180 degrees out of phase with the direction of movement, so it feels heavier. Once past that point, the pull of resistance rapidly drops off, and near the end of the movement it becomes nearly zero.

The weight seems to change during a curl. This apparent change is a result of challenging a rotary movement with a straight-line source of resistance. The biceps muscles, the muscles worked during a curl, receive heavy resistance only during a very limited part of the movement. But during the rest of the movement the resistance is far too light.

For full-range exercise the body part that is being moved by muscular contraction must be rotating on a common axis with the source of resistance. In effect, the joint, the elbow joint in the case of a curl, must be in line with the axis of a rotary form of resistance. When this arrangement of axis points is correct the resistance is always exactly 180 degrees out of phase with

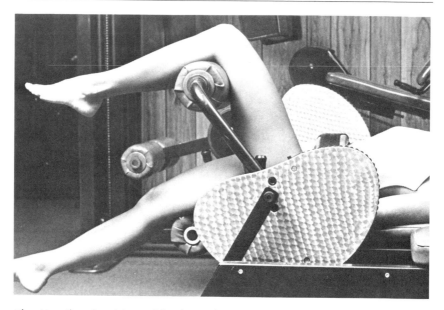

The Nautilus duo hip and back machine provides rotary resistance for the major muscles of the buttocks. When positioned properly in this machine, the hip joints should be in line with the axes of the cams. (Photo by Scott LeGear)

the momentary direction of movement. You are always lifting the weight, regardless of your actual direction of movement.

Without such rotary-form resistance, full-range exercise is impossible. And Nautilus training provides that resistance.

POSITIVE WORK

When you lift a weight you're performing positive work. Your muscles are producing movement by concentric contraction, reducing their length.

Almost all forms of exercise involve positive work, even if movement of the resistance is not produced. But some forms of exercise demand only positive work.

Within the last several years much has been claimed for a form of exercise called *isokinetics*. But, as stated earlier, this form is limited to positive work, and all such exercises are based on friction of one kind or another.

A positive-only style of training could be produced with a barbell in either of two ways: (1) You could lift a barbell, immediately drop it upon reaching the top position of movement, then lift it again, then drop it again. (2) With the help of assistants, you could lift the barbell and have them take it from you as soon as it reaches the top position and lower it back down for you. (The assistants performed the negative part of the work in this case.)

Such a style of training with a barbell would be very dangerous in the first instance and impractical in the second. It would be only slightly effective in either case because a positive-only form of exercise is lacking several of the requirements for productive exercise. Positive work is certainly of value in exercise, but positive-only exercise suffers from numerous limitations.

NEGATIVE WORK

When you lower a weight you're performing negative work. Your muscles are limiting movement by eccentric contraction while increasing their length.

If a barbell is dropped from the top position, then negative work is not performed. The normal downward movement of the resistance produced by gravity must be limited to force negative work. Normal acceleration must be prevented; movement must be slowed and controlled.

A negative-only style of training can be provided in several ways: (1) Assistants can lift the weight for you so that you limit your efforts to lowering the weight slowly. (2) Climb onto a chair into the top position of a chinning exercise and limit the exercise to a negative-only style by lowering yourself from the top position. (3) Use a mechanical arrangement that lifts the weight so that you can lower it. The first style is impractical, because of the need for helpers. The second is limited to certain exercises: chinning, dipping, and a few others. The third style requires special equipment.

But do note that the negative part of movement is one of the most important parts of exercise. In fact, it is probably the most important part performed for the purpose of increasing strength. To the degree that it is possible under the prevailing circumstances, the negative part of exercise should be emphasized as much as possible.

Many people make the mistake of paying close attention to

Isokinetic machines do not supply negative work to the involved muscles.

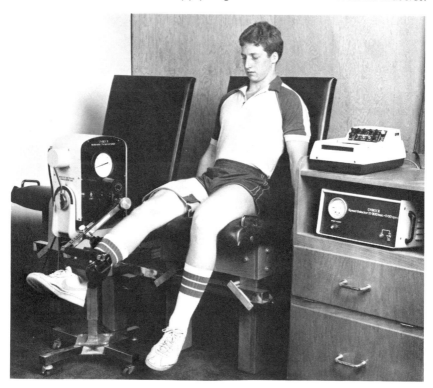

the positive part of their exercises but ignore the negative part. They lift the weight smoothly and in good form, then lower it in a haphazard manner. Thus, they deny themselves a large part of the potential benefits of their exercises. You should lift the weight in a smooth, steady motion, without pause and without jerking or sudden movement. Then lower the weight in the same fashion, smoothly, steadily, and even more slowly.

Negative work is possible only when there is a source of back pressure, a force pulling in a direction opposite to the direction of movement produced by muscular contraction. During barbell exercises the muscles are pulling up and the force of gravity is pulling down. So a barbell provides both positive and negative work.

But the friction-based type of exercise, isokinetics, does not provide negative work. There is no back pressure of force pulling the muscles back toward the starting position. In such exercises resistance is provided only while you're moving in a positive direction. If movement stops, the resistance stops.

Lacking back pressure for negative work, such exercises consequently also fail to fill several other requirements for productive exercises. Prior to the start of movement there is no back pressure or force to pull the joints into a stretched position, and no force to prestretch the muscles before the start of contraction. Thus isokinetic exercise does nothing for flexibility. Flexibility requires stretching. Neither does isokinetic exercise provide a high intensity of muscular contraction, which also requires prestretching.

STRETCHING

A relaxed arm does not hang in a fully straightened position. It tends to remain slightly bent. The biceps that bend the arm and the triceps that straighten the arm are always pulling slightly in opposite directions.

You can straighten your arm by contracting the triceps while attempting to relax the biceps as much as possible. But you cannot stretch the biceps without an external source of force.

Stretching is provided in most Nautilus machines. Here, the pectoralis major muscles are being stretched on the 50° chest/shoulder machine.

If such stretching is not a regular part of your exercises, you'll gradually reduce your degree of flexibility. At the same time you'll lose the ability to move into positions that were previously possible.

Young children are normally very flexible, but as they grow older they lose much of that flexibility. This is partially unavoidable, since some of a child's flexibility results from the fact that his bones are soft and his limbs are fairly thin. Both are factors that change with age. But a certain part of the flexibility loss that occurs between childhood and maturity is the direct result of failing to stretch. Some of the athletic injuries that happen every year are caused by the unnatural loss of normal flexibility.

A low level of strength can be maintained with no systematic exercise. An apparently normal range of movement can also be maintained without exercise. But without proper exercise, losses in both strength and flexibility will progress steadily until a person becomes far weaker and much less flexible than ever suspected.

Some barbell exercises improve flexibility; others do not,

depending on the degree of stretching involved. Exercises performed on a Universal Gym generally provide less stretching than similar barbell exercises, primarily because the resistance is supported in the starting position. And isokinetic exercises, because they involve no stretching, do absolutely nothing for flexibility.

PRESTRETCHING

Prestretching is a natural reflex that brings about a protective response from the muscle. When properly applied, prestretching stimulates a potentially higher intensity of muscular contraction.

Examples of prestretching occur in many human movements: the slight dip just before a basketball player jumps for a rebound; the backswing of the batter; the quick, backward arm movement of a boxer preparing to punch.

Prestretching is possible in all human movements by reversing the direction of bodily movement just before starting the move in the intended direction. The potential for prestretching supplied by any exercise device depends on the quality of negative work potential provided by the apparatus.

Prestretching is often confused with stretching. Prestretching has nothing to do with stretching except that it should occur before the stretch to prevent overstretching and injury. Perhaps a better term for this phenomenon is *precontraction*.

Prestretching is probably not necessary for full-range exercise. In fact, it is more abused than properly used. That's why in teaching Nautilus to most beginners, and especially when using the super-slow technique (which will be described in Chapter 8), the emphasis is on a gradual movement rather than a sudden thrust. Super-slow training is best accomplished without resorting to prestretching. If prestretching is used, it is most safely applied during the last one or two repetitions of an exercise.

Barbell, Universal Gym, and Nautilus machine exercises provide prestretching. Isokinetic devices do not provide prestretching, since they offer no negative work.

AUTOMATICALLY VARIABLE RESISTANCE

Muscles are not equally strong in all positions, and movement produces changes in the mechanical efficiency of the joints involved. As a result of these two factors, you're much stronger in some positions than in others. If the resistance remains constant in all positions, it will be correct in only one position and too light in all other positions throughout a full range of possible movement.

You're actually limited to the amount of resistance that you can handle in your weakest position. If you try to use more resistance, you'll find it impossible to move it through the weakest area of movement.

In practice some variation in available resistance occurs in almost all exercises, even though the actual weight of the resistance remains constant. In the barbell curl we discussed earlier there is no available resistance in either the starting or finishing position of the exercise. There is also a constant change in resistance as the movement occurs, since the arms moving the resistance change in relation to gravity. But such variations in resistance are random in nature and have no relationship to the ability of the muscles to handle resistance in a particular position.

If a rotary-form curling machine is built with a round pulley directly in line with the elbow joints, the resistance will remain exactly the same throughout the full range of possible movement. It will not feel the same, however. Instead, as noted, it will feel very heavy at the start of the movement. Once you are moving, the weight seems to become lighter. Later in the movement it will seem ridiculously light. Finally, at the end of the movement the weight will begin to feel heavier again. All this is deceiving and is not based on the simple facts of muscle physiology.

The resistance in a barbell curl starts at zero, then increases rapidly to peak resistance after 90 degrees of movement. It then plummets back to zero near the end of the curl. So the resistance in a barbell curl starts off too low, increases too rapidly, and ceases too soon.

Changing from a barbell curl to a rotary-form curling machine does not solve the problem. The level of resistance in the various positions throughout the movement is still not in accord with the available strength in the same positions. In a barbell curl the available resistance changes, but it changes too fast and too much. In a rotary-form curling machine the resistance does not change at all—but it should.

The problem of these extremes is solved by the Nautilus cam. Instead of a round pulley, Nautilus machines use a spiral pulley, so that the resistance changes instantly and automatically as a movement occurs and available strength changes. Physics and muscle physiology, therefore, dictated the design of the Nautilus cams.

At the start of a curl in a Nautilus biceps curling machine the radius of the pulley is fairly small. In that position you're not as strong as you will be later in the movement. The machine gives you a mechanical advantage in that position. As you move into a stronger position, the radius of the pulley changes, becoming larger or smaller as it must to accommodate the level of strength available in every position.

BALANCED RESISTANCE

Having automatically variable resistance is not enough. The resistance must be varied and, in effect, balanced in accordance with your potential strength in all positions.

The exact size and shape of the cam is crucial. It must provide as much resistance as you can handle in each position, but no more. While several small companies are now illegally trying to copy the Nautilus cams, so far they do not have even an elementary understanding of the cam's required shape. Having a cam is not enough. It must be the right cam for the particular application. Fords and Chevrolets both have cams. But a Chevrolet cam will not survive in a Ford, and vice versa.

So cams, correctly designed for each large muscle group, are required to balance the resistance in relation to any particular person's available strength.

DIRECT RESISTANCE

Muscular contraction produces direct movement of the body part to which the muscle is attached. During a curl the contraction of the biceps results in movement of the forearm. The hand, which is attached to the forearm, also moves, but indirectly rather than directly.

For direct application, the resistance must be applied to the actual body part that is attached to and directly moved by contraction of the muscle you're trying to work. In a curl this means that the resistance would have to be applied against the forearm instead of the hand.

In an actual curl, though, such direct application of resistance is of little importance. The relative strength of the curling muscles is not out of proportion to the strength of the

The 10° chest machine by-passes the weaker muscles that extend the forearms and places the resistance directly on the upper arms.

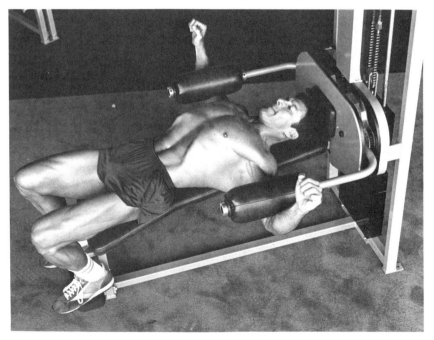

forearm muscles involved in keeping the hand straight in line with the forearm during a curl. So in this case other muscles do not limit your curling ability, even though the resistance is not applied directly.

In most exercises the resistance must be applied directly to overcome the limitation of other, weaker muscles. Exercises designed for the large muscles of the torso suffer severely from indirect application of the resistance. Since the muscles of the arms are also involved in these exercises, the exertion must end when the arm muscles are exhausted. This exhaustion occurs long before the larger, stronger muscles of the torso have been worked heavily enough for best results.

Chinning-type exercises, for instance, are performed primarily to work the larger muscles of the upper torso. But these exercises also involve the bending muscles of the arms. As a consequence, the relatively low strength of the arm muscles results in poor exercise for the torso muscles. Your exhausted arms force you to stop the exercise before your torso muscles have been worked properly.

To work the torso muscles correctly, the resistance must be applied directly to the body part that is actually attached to and moved by the muscles of the torso. In practice the resistance must be applied directly against the upper arms. What happens to the forearms and hands during the exercise is not important if the forearms and hands do not get in the way of the movement. And in a Nautilus pullover machine the resistance is applied directly against your upper arms. The large muscles of the torso can be worked directly without the limitations imposed by smaller and weaker muscles.

Most barbell exercises and most barbell-like exercises performed on a Universal Gym do not provide such direct resistance. Isokinetic exercises, in general, suffer from the same limitations. There are a few exceptions in all these machines: a curl is a direct exercise regardless of how it is performed; a wrist curl is a direct exercise; and so are leg extensions and leg curls. But in general, direct exercise is provided best by Nautilus equipment.

Transposition

Transposition is the conversion of straight-line force to a rotational force or vice versa. The force of gravity at any point on the surface of the earth is perpetually downward. It is vertical. Upward movement is directly opposed to gravity; downward movement moves with the direction of gravity. Alternately upward and downward movement reciprocates, just as do the pistons in most internal combustion engines.

The weight stack serially depicted in the illustrations produces a downward force. Since the force is always downward, it is said to be unidirectional. A chain attached to the weight stack is wound around and anchored to the far side of a four-inch pulley. The pulley is fused to a handle that is five inches long.

If we ignore the weight of the chain and the inherent friction about the pulley's axis, torque can be calculated.

The clockwise torque produced at the pulley's axis is 100 pounds times 4 inches, or 400 inch-pounds.

To calculate the required counterclockwise force to balance the clockwise torque, we equate force $\times$ lever length = force $\times$ lever length. Therefore, $100 \times 4 = 400 = 5 \times F$. F, then, equals 80 pounds.

In all positions 80 pounds must be applied to the handle to balance the axial torque. But note that the instantaneous direction of the handle is to the left in the first position. It is upward in the second, to the right in the third, and downward in the fourth position. The handle rotates, and its instantaneous direction is different in every position. The straight-line force of the weight stack is transposed to an omnidirectional or rotational force at the handle.

Though impossible, the perfect exercise machine would first remove the muscle from the body and then apply balanced straight-line resistance from a full stretch to full muscular contraction. But since the body transposes straight-line muscular function to the rotary action of the joints, the most efficient approach is to match rotary function with rotary resistance.

—Ken Hutchins

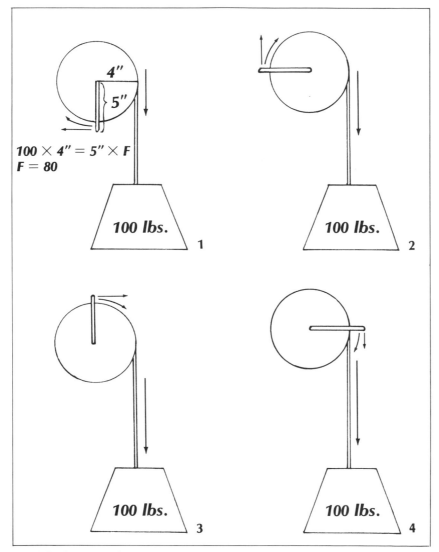

$$100 \times 4'' = 5'' \times F$$
$$F = 80$$

RESISTANCE IN THE POSITION OF FULL MUSCULAR CONTRACTION

Full muscular contraction occurs in a position where additional movement is impossible. Obviously, an isokinetic form of exercise provides no work in the finishing position of an exercise. Isokinetic exercises provide resistance from friction, and friction is produced by movement. When movement stops, friction stops. Without friction there is no resistance, and without resistance there is no exercise. In isokinetic exercise there is no back pressure of negative work pulling against the muscles and, therefore, no exercise in the finishing position of full muscular contraction.

Neither do most barbell exercises or most Universal Gym exercises provide work in the finishing position. In most of these exercises the body parts are locked out under the resistance and the weight is supported entirely by the bones. Such lock-outs occur during all major barbell exercises and in all major Universal Gym exercises such as curls, all forms of pressing, squats, leg presses, and many other exercises. In these exercises there is no effective resistance at the end of the movement. The lever arm of the resistance is reduced to zero, and no resistance is being applied to the muscles.

But there are exceptions. A few minor barbell exercises and Universal Gym exercises do provide resistance in the finishing position. Some such exceptions are wrist curls, calf raises, and shoulder shrugs.

UNRESTRICTED SPEED OF MOVEMENT

In exercise the speed of movement should not be limited. But since speed is limited in isokinetic forms of exercise, these exercises are insufficient.

At the start of an isokinetic form of exercise there is no resistance until the person's speed of movement reaches the preset speed of movement on the machine. There is obviously no resistance at the start of the isokinetic movement. And at the end of an isokinetic exercise, when any speed of movement is impossible, there is again no resistance. Isokinetic exercises are based on friction that limits the speed of movement. This can be accomplished through the use of an inertia-reel or a hydraulic cylinder and perhaps in a few more ways, but the result is much the same no matter what the means.

The actual speed of movement during a properly performed exercise should vary. During the first few repetitions the speed should be fairly slow and constant, without jerking. During later repetitions, as the muscles become tired, the speed should be slightly faster, but jerking must still be avoided. Finally, as the muscles reach a point of momentary exhaustion, the speed of movement should be very slow.

The speed of movement in barbell exercises and in Universal Gym exercises is not limited, so these exercises do not suffer from this limitation. Neither is the speed of movement limited in Nautilus exercises.

THE SUPERIORITY OF NAUTILUS

Ridiculous claims are being widely advertised for a number of forms of exercise. Almost all such exercises are supposedly full-range. But once you understand the facts, you can see these false claims in proper perspective. If an exercise is lacking any one of the ten basic requirements, it cannot be a full-range exercise, no matter what the claims of uninformed promoters.

Most barbell and many machine exercises satisfy only four of the ten requirements: positive work, negative work, pre-stretching, and unrestricted speed of movement. Isokinetic exercise machines generally provide only one of the basic requirements: positive work. But Nautilus single-joint rotary machines fulfill all ten requirements.

When the requirements for full-range exercise are understood and applied in a practical fashion it becomes possible to devise a form of exercise that involves a muscle's entire structure. Only Nautilus machines make it possible to involve the whole muscular structure: the related body parts, the joints, the connective tissue, and even the bones. Such total exercise is capable of producing a level of strength and fitness that cannot be duplicated in any other fashion. Nautilus is the only form of exercise that is tailored to the requirements and limitations of the body itself.

Having a machine with a cam is not enough for quality exercise. The cam and many other factors must be correct for the involved muscles. The above machine, built by a manufacturing company that is no longer in business, is an example of "how *not* to build an exercise device." The cam is shaped wrong, the axis of rotation of the machine is located two inches below the elbows, and the hand grips are twisted in the opposite direction.

6

The Nautilus Cam

The Nautilus spiral pulley or cam is the hallmark of Nautilus. What is the cam? Why is it so important?

According to the dictionary, a cam is "a lobed shaft that rotates, thereby increasing and decreasing its radius at a critical point to depress alternately a pushrod." This is the cam shaft assembly familiar to automobile mechanics. Its original design is much older than the automobile.

The cam principle dates back to the use of waterwheels in the beer industry in approximately 890 A.D. Waterwheels were used for many purposes. One was to power a turning cam shaft. The cam lobes bumped trip-hammers. Later, the same applications were used in the textile industry and the iron industry. Cams became very common in the various machines of the Industrial Revolution.

As portable timepieces were developed during the fifteenth century, the fusee was invented. The fusee is a spindle-shaped

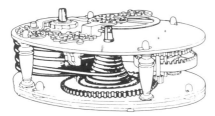

The insides of a spring-driven clock are shown here. The cone-shaped fusee is in the middle of the drawing. The fusee's function is similar to that of the Nautilus cam.

wheel on the main drive of a spring-driven clock. As the spring unwinds, it becomes weaker, but its force is maintained by the fusee's increasing radius. This application closely resembles the Nautilus cam.

The Nautilus cam is more accurately defined as an eccentric pulley or wheel at the end of a drive shaft. It has a timed lobe or increased radius. Since it does not depress a pushrod, its function is not exactly that of a true cam. But it does deserve the same name. The cam is used on a Nautilus machine to vary the resistance in exercise properly.

Resistance can be varied by different mechanical applications. The only practical way, however, is with the use of the Nautilus cam.

HOW DOES THE CAM WORK?

The Nautilus cam varies torque about a rotational axis. Torque is twisting force. Torque is the product of two factors: perpendicular force and leverage. Leverage or lever length is also known as *moment* or *moment arm.*

If a 100-pound force is applied perpendicularly to an axis of rotation and the perpendicular distance from the axis is 10 inches, then the torque is 1,000 inch-pounds. If the lever (perpendicular distance from the axis) is doubled, then the torque doubles. If the lever is zero, then the torque is zero, no matter what force is applied perpendicularly.

The radius of the cam changes. This change is timed to the positional strength of the working body part. As the body part becomes stronger, the cam radius increases; thus the effective

lever increases, providing the body with automatically increased torque or effective resistance.

As the body part moves into a position of potential weakness, the cam radius decreases, providing less resistance.

The description so far has been for a positive cam.

Nautilus also makes use of another type of cam: a negative

Shown is a close-up of
the positive cam on the
biceps curl of the plate-
loading biceps/triceps
machine. As the arms
bend, the cam winds the
chain around its radius.

The cam used on the
overhead press of the
double shoulder machine
is a negative cam. As the
resistance bar is pressed
overhead, the cam
unwinds.

cam. With a positive cam, larger is heavier. With a negative cam, smaller is heavier.

A positive cam winds. A negative cam unwinds.

Positive cams are applicable in single-joint rotary machines.

Negative cams are best used in machines that provide compound movements, such as the duo squat, behind neck pulldown, and overhead press.

Where the muscle is stronger, the cam reduces mechanical advantage. Where the muscle is weaker, the cam increases mechanical advantage. Just like the seesaw at the playground, the heavier boy perfectly balances against the lighter by using respectively shorter and longer lengths of the teeter-totter. The cam performs essentially the same function for the muscles.

SIMPLE VERSUS COMPOUND MOVEMENTS

A simple movement on a Nautilus machine involves rotation around one joint. Examples of machines providing simple movements are the leg extension, lateral raise, and triceps extension.

A compound movement necessitates rotation around two or more joints. The duo squat and decline press involve compound movements.

The inherent differences between compound and simple movements take on more importance as the proper resistance curve is determined.

The changes in potential strength in a simple movement are not dramatic. For instance, there is no position where the muscle is two or three times stronger than in another position. The cam is constructed to vary the resistance between 40 and 50 percent. This is meaningful and important to the efficiency of the exercise, but in no way can it compare to the enormous positional changes that occur in a compound movement. The resistance of a simple movement is virtually flat when compared to the curve of a compound movement.

The major determinant of strength variation in a simple

movement is the changing insertion angles of the involved muscles. For this reason, the Nautilus resistance curve in a simple movement is extremely efficient. Rotary-based Nautilus machines approach an efficiency of 100 percent and are equally valid for all people.

On the other hand, the major determinant of strength variation in a compound movement is the wide range of possible bone lengths. The resulting output of the body part involves the output of several different muscle systems plus an enormous variation in leverage. This change in leverage far exceeds the change from the muscles alone. This is why the Nautilus duo squat machine does not provide as much resistance as the muscles actually need at or near lock-out. It provides only what the bones and joints can stand. Referring to the muscle requirements exclusively, the perfect resistance curve would crush the skeleton.

Compound movements in Nautilus equipment are necessarily less efficient than rotary-based Nautilus exercises. And due to individual differences in leverage and limb length, the curve is not exactly the same for all individuals. Recent innovations at the Nautilus laboratories solved this problem in some compound movements, but the solutions are not yet practical.

VARIABLE RESISTANCE NOT NEW

As noted in Chapter 5, variable resistance is a requirement for full-range exercise. Variable resistance is not new or even unique to a Nautilus machine.

The first Nautilus pullover machine was made in 1948. A series of attempts produced a design that resembles the modern production model. It had a major flaw, however.

In discovering the importance of rotary and direct resistance, Arthur Jones inadvertently removed variable resistance. He used circular pulley wheels (with a constant radius) on the machine's rotational shafts. The resistance remained constant throughout a full range of possible movement.

One of Arthur Jones's first attempts at building a metal Nautilus machine sits in storage at Nautilus Sports/Medical Industries. You'll notice that the cams of these two facing pullover machines are round. Before Jones hit upon the idea of using spiral pulleys to vary the resistance, he used large circular wheels that were connected to cables that were attached to piles of chain. As the wheels rotated, more chains were lifted and the resistance became progressively heavier.

There was another, though slight, source of resistance variation. This variation was not due to the apparatus. It was due to a changing leverage in the related body parts. The mass, mass distribution, and length of the arms produced an unbalanced torque as they rotated. This variation was backward for the most part. The weight of the arms decreased the resistance at just the point when an increase in resistance is desirable. Had the machine been designed to rotate in a horizontal plane on a vertical axis, then variation of the resistance would have been zero.

This antique provided valuable answers to Jones. With this nonvarying pullover, it was possible to demonstrate how important variable resistance is to exercise.

For instance, if a man was provided with a moderately heavy resistance in the contracted position, he found that it became heavier to the point of dislocating his shoulders as he allowed them to stretch backward. The resistance did not meaningfully change due to the weight of his arms, and it didn't change at all due to the machine's mechanics. The resistance became too heavy because the muscle is weaker in its stretched position. This showed that variable resistance is required.

The important point is that, though variable resistance is usually unavoidable, most exercises vary resistance improperly. Resistance is almost never in the correct proportion to the potential strength in every position for the muscle intended. Conventional exercise tools don't lack variable resistance. They lack resistance that is balanced according to your potential strength curve.

ESTABLISHING A STRENGTH CURVE

Many factors are involved with the determination of the strength curve for any given muscular structure. Some of them are:

1. Predictable tension/length curves for specific muscular structures

2. The degree of overlapping muscular involvement in different positions of movement
3. The efficiency of tendon insertion angle
4. Leverage changes in the body

These factors must be integrated in a logical manner to derive the proper resistance curve for an exercise device. This is applied by the cam in a Nautilus machine. But several interrelated mechanical factors must be satisfied before the cam can perform its job properly.

When solving simultaneous equations in math classes, we learned that it is necessary to make the equations equal to the same value, preferably zero. When designing a Nautilus machine, it is also necessary to cancel out the random resistance—to make all values equal so that only one variable is dealt with. The movement arms on a Nautilus machine must first be perfectly counterbalanced to create zero torque in all positions of rotation. Only then is it possible to establish accurately the intended strength curve with the profile of the cam. This being so, there are other considerations.

There is a precise relationship among these four factors in a Nautilus machine:

1. The general size and shape of the cam
2. The radius of the first redirectional sprocket
3. The angle between the cam axis and the axis of the first redirectional sprocket
4. The distance from the cam axis to the axis of the first redirectional sprocket

Once these factors are determined properly for the correct resistance curve in a Nautilus machine, changing any one of them results in incorrect values for the other three.

A story is told about a man from Tampa who visited Nautilus Sports/Medical Industries in 1970, supposedly to apply for a job. "If only I could steal a Nautilus cam," he thought. He sincerely believed that he was going to make off with the Holy

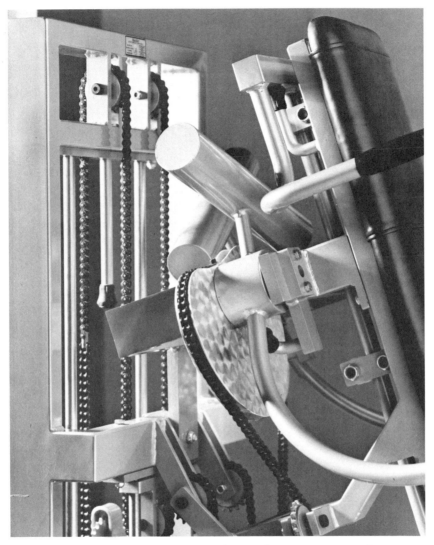

The lateral raise of the double shoulder machine requires two heavy counterweights to balance the weight of the movement arms. The counterweights are criss crossed in the middle of the above picture.

Grail of exercise. He pilfered an early ribbed cam, as most of them were in those days. Of course he had no notion whatsoever of the delicate interrelationships mentioned in the previous paragraph. He didn't even know for which machine the cam was intended, much less have any idea that he might require additional information.

CRITICS OF THE CAM

Since the emergence of Nautilus machines, *variable resistance* has become the buzzword of exercise equipment advertising. Many manufacturers apparently believe or want the public to believe that variable resistance is the sole ingredient of a sophisticated exercise machine.

It is seldom suspected that almost all exercise involves variable resistance. Again, what fitness seekers need is *balanced resistance.* As important as it is, balanced resistance is only one of ten requirements of full-range exercise. These other requirements are further predicated upon restricted movement according to muscular function.

At various fitness conventions staff members of Nautilus Sports/Medical Industries have met a few professed experts of exercise and competing equipment designers who say the Nautilus cams are wrong, that the resulting resistance curves are incorrect for some of the exercises. Again, they invariably demonstrate an ignorance of the required mechanical and engineering factors. Among many misconceptions, they often recommend designs that defy muscular function, usually trying to mimic the movements of some popular sport.

We are no longer surprised to find that many would-be experts possess total ignorance of some of the principles in this book. Exposing them to the correct information is often to no avail, since they apparently are unable to put their preconceptions aside and listen to modern concepts objectively.

We have great confidence in the Nautilus cam profiles. But let's consider the unlikely event that a cam is wrong. Let's suppose that a rotary-based Nautilus machine is delivered to a

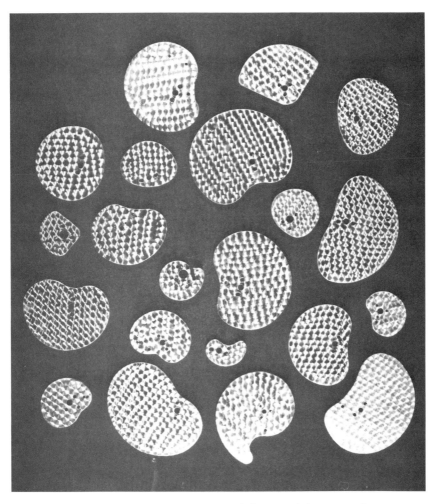

This picture reveals some of the sizes and shapes of the more than two dozen Nautilus cams. Each muscle group in your body has a potential strength curve that is different from those of other muscle groups. Thus, scientifically-designed cams are incorporated into specific Nautilus machines to compensate for those differences.

customer that has no cam at all. It has only a circular pulley drive.

If the resulting flat resistance curve is wrong for the intended muscle group and all the other requirements for full-range exercise are provided and muscular function is tracked closely, then how great is the actual compromise?

An incorrect resistance curve will greatly compromise the efficiency of any Nautilus machine, but the general exercise effect of the machine will still be light-years ahead of any other device. Arguing the correct strength curve is splitting hairs when many of the other requirements are left out, as is the case with most conventional exercise devices.

Nautilus machine design is continuously evolving to provide increased efficiency. *If* the cams in Nautilus machines can be improved a few percentage points, Nautilus will discover the required change. No one else presently possesses either the required information or the necessary tensiometers for making such determinations.

Cams Within Cams

Some of the differences between the positive cam and the negative cam have already been mentioned. It is also possible to have a cam effect in a mechanical system without the presence of a literal cam.

As you perform a biceps curl with a dumbbell, the dumbbell produces a positive cam effect on your muscle. We define this effect as positive, since the resistance increases as the effective lever—the distance from the dumbbell to the axis of your elbow—increases.

In 1985, Nautilus researchers discovered that there are negative cam effects working within the human body. In fact, your whole musculoskeletal system is a series of negative cam effects. Note the biceps tendon in the first two diagrams. The effective lever is the perpendicular distance from the tendon to the axis of the elbow. As the elbow is flexed, the effective lever changes. An increase in effective lever reduces resistance against the muscle. A decrease in effective lever increases resistance. The biceps tendon, therefore, produces a negative cam effect on your biceps.

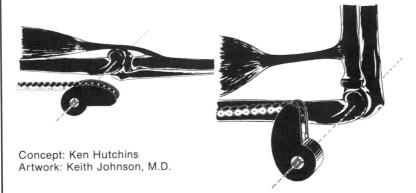

Concept: Ken Hutchins
Artwork: Keith Johnson, M.D.

Nature's application of positive and negative cam effects in the body does not stop here. Looking deep inside the muscle, microscopic filaments slide past one another to produce what we experience as the overall muscle contraction. The action is a telescopic movement of alternately interlaced fibers respectively called actin and myosin. Each myosin filament is the foundation for thousands of minute cross-bridges. During contraction, each cross-bridge extends to an active site on a neighboring actin filament, then flexes to telescope the actin along the myosin filament. The end result is that the overall length of the muscle shortens.

The cross-bridges in a sense are appendages—like your arms and legs. They have joints and, as we have seen, can extend and flex.

Some as yet unidentified force inside the angle of the joint of the cross-bridge offsets a negative cam effect, producing flexion. This is the same mechanical arrangement witnessed as your biceps flexes your lower arm bone.

Cross-bridge flexion is produced against a positive cam effect. This positive cam effect is due to the actin filament's resistance on the distal end of the cross-bridge. It is likened to the positive cam effect of the dumbbell against your lower arm bone.

To put all of this information in context, study the following schematic:

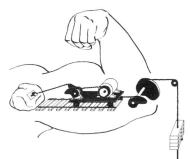

Concept: Ken Hutchins
Artwork: Keith Johnson, M.D.

Try to identify the four cam effects represented:

1. Negative cam effect—inside angle of cross-bridge joint.
2. Positive cam effect—distal end of the cross-bridge.
3. Negative cam effect—inside angle of elbow.
4. Positive cam effect—on the lower arm bone due to a barbell, pulley machine, or a literal positive or negative Nautilus cam.

Thus, from a mechanical point of view, the human body effectively functions as a cam within a cam within a cam.

7

Nautilus Training Principles

While Nautilus equipment makes it possible to benefit dramatically from exercise, it does not offer easy results. Full-range exercise performed on Nautilus machines is demanding. It is by far the hardest recognized form of exercise. It happens fast, and it's enormously productive. But it was never intended to be easy.

Arthur Jones developed the hardest possible form of exertion by involving maximum possible muscle fibers in each exercise movement. If you want fast results, rest assured that properly performed Nautilus machine exercises will produce them more quickly than any other equipment. This statement sounds bold, but it's scientifically true.

A clear understanding of the following principles will assure you the best possible results from Nautilus machines.

INTENSITY

The building of strength is proportionate to the intensity of exercise. The higher the intensity, the better the muscles are stimulated. Performing a Nautilus exercise to the point of momentary muscular failure assures that you've trained to maximum intensity. Muscular failure means that no additional repetitions are possible. Only by working to this extent can you engage a maximum number of muscle fibers.

The first few repetitions on a Nautilus machine are merely preparation, doing little to increase strength. These repetitions are of limited value because the intensity is low. The final repetitions are productive because the intensity is high.

Many people refuse to perform these last several repetitions. But those forced repetitions are the most effective. A Nautilus exercise should not be considered completed until you just can't perform another repetition in correct form.

When you can perform more than 12 repetitions on a Nautilus machine, that is the signal to increase the resistance by 5 percent at the next workout. Unless you are using over 200 pounds on a machine, that progression in resistance is best made by the addition of small saddle plates to the top of the weight stack.

PROGRESSION

The cornerstone of Nautilus training is progression. Progression means attempting to increase the workload during every training session. With each workout you should try to add another repetition, increase resistance, or both. Experience has shown that at least 8 repetitions should be performed and not more than 12. If you cannot achieve 8 repetitions, the resistance is too heavy. If you can perform more than 12 repetitions, it is too light. When you can perform 12 repetitions or more it is time to increase the resistance on that Nautilus machine by approximately 5 percent at the next workout.

Nautilus machines are made with 10-pound weight increments. But Nautilus also manufactures small saddle plates weighing 1¼, 2½, 5, and 7½ pounds that, when correctly added to the top plate of a machine, will allow you to progress in a systematic manner.

FORM

The style of performance is very important if maximum benefit is to be obtained from a Nautilus training program. Proper form includes both speed and range of movement.

Repetitions performed in a slow, smooth manner apply steady force throughout the entire movement. Fast repetitions apply force to only a small portion at the beginning and the end of the movement. When a resistance is jerked or thrown, three or four times the actual force required to move the resistance is directed at the joints and muscles. This is both ineffective and dangerous.

The range of movement of each repetition, from full extension to full flexion, should be as great as possible. To contract at all, a muscle must produce movement. To contract fully, however, a muscle must produce a full range of movement. If the movement resulting from muscular contraction is less than full-range, the entire length of the muscle is not involved in the work. Improved performance and prevention of injury are most likely when the muscles have been strengthened in every position over a full range of possible movement.

ACCENTUATE THE NEGATIVE

For best results, each repetition should be performed in a negative-emphasized manner. The performance of Nautilus exercise requires the raising and lowering of resistance. When you raise the weight stack you're moving against the resistance of gravity and performing positive work. Lowering a weight under control brings gravity into play in another fashion and is termed *negative work*.

In a Nautilus biceps curl you perform both positive and negative work during each repetition. Positive resistance is involved when the arms are bending and raising the weight. Negative resistance comes into play when the arms straighten and lower the weight. Up is positive; down is negative. This is true for each Nautilus machine.

Dr. Paavo Komi of Finland and other physiologists have determined that, for strength-building purposes, the negative part of an exercise has much more value than the positive portion. Nautilus machines are more productive when ways are devised to accentuate the negative part of each movement.

In normal positive-negative exercise performed on Nautilus equipment you should always concentrate on the lowering part of the movement. If it takes two seconds to lift a weight smoothly, it should take about four seconds to lower it.

To perform negative-only exercise, you need to select a heavier weight than you would normally use. Initially, you should use about 40 percent more weight than you can handle for 10 repetitions in a normal positive-negative manner. With this additional amount of weight on the Nautilus machine, you have one or two assistants, or instructors, lift the movement arm to the contracted position. It is then your job to lower the resistance back to the starting position.

During the first two or three repetitions it should take

Negative-only chins can be performed on the multi-exercise machine by climbing into the top position with the legs and lowering slowly to the bottom positon with the arms.

approximately 8–10 seconds per repetition to lower the resistance in a slow, even manner. It should be possible for you to stop and reverse the movement of these repetitions, though no attempt should be made to do so.

If the weight has been selected correctly, the middle three or four repetitions should be performed slightly faster, approximately four to five seconds per repetition. In these repetitions you should be able to stop the movement but not reverse it.

During the last repetition it becomes impossible to stop the downward movement, even though you can control it. The exercise is finally terminated when the downward movement can no longer be controlled.

Properly performed, negative-only exercise is a very effective style of Nautilus training. But there are problems, since it is usually necessary to have someone lift the movement arm for you.

A few exercises can be performed in a negative-only manner without help. Negative chins and dips on the multi-exercise machine can be done by climbing into the top position with the legs and slowly lowering with the arms. Thus, your lower body is doing the positive work and your upper body is doing the negative work. This style of training can also be performed on four older Nautilus machines, called Omni. In most cases, a foot-pedal attachment allows you to leg-press the movement arm into the contracted position and lower the resistance with your upper body. But since your upper body is weaker than your lower body, you cannot work your lower body in this fashion. That is why negative-accentuated training was invented.

Negative-accentuated training does not require helpers. Nor does it require nearly as much resistance as negative-only training. You can use Nautilus machines that have single connected movement arms.

The leg extension machine offers a good example of negative-accentuated exercise. If you can handle 100 pounds for 10 repetitions in a normal manner, you should use 70 pounds here—in other words, 70 percent of the weight you normally handle.

The movement arm should be lifted with both legs. Pause in the contracted position and smoothly transfer the resistance from both legs to the right leg. Then slowly lower the resistance in about eight seconds, using only the right leg. Lift it back to the top position with both legs, pause, and lower this time with the left leg, again in a slow, even manner. Up with two, down with one, up with two again, down with the other. Continue this until you can no longer raise the weight to the contracted position.

If the weight is selected correctly, you should reach a point of momentary failure at about the eleventh or twelfth lifting repetition. When you can perform 12 repetitions, increase the resistance by 5 percent. A properly performed set of negative-accentuated exercises should consist of 8–12 lifting movements, plus 4–6 negative movements performed by the right leg and an equal number by the left.

Other negative-accentuated exercises that can be performed on various machines are the leg curl, leg press, calf raise, pullover, overhead press, decline press, biceps curl, and triceps extension.

DURATION

If each Nautilus exercise is done properly in a high-intensity fashion, brief workouts must be the rule. High-intensity exercise has an effect on the entire system that can be either good or bad; low-intensity work has almost no effect at all. If high-intensity work is followed by an adequate period of rest, muscular growth and increase in strength will result. Intensive work, however, must not be overdone.

Many athletes mistakenly perform too much exercise. They do too many different movements, too many sets, and too many workouts within a given period of time. When an excess amount of Nautilus exercise is performed, total recovery between workouts becomes impossible. So does high-intensity training.

You can perform brief and infrequent high-intensity exercise or long and frequent low-intensity workouts. But you cannot perform long and frequent Nautilus exercise involving a high intensity of work. That will result only in losses in both muscular mass and strength. It can also result in total exhaustion.

Understanding the requirements for a productive style of high-intensity exercise allows selection of the best exercises for a particular purpose. In most cases not more than 12 different Nautilus exercises should be performed in any one workout. The lower body should have 4–6 exercises and the upper body 6–8. If you push or are pushed to the supreme effort in each of 12 exercises, you will not be able to perform more than one set properly.

A set of 10 repetitions performed in proper style should take about one minute to complete. Allowing one minute between exercises, most athletes should be able to complete 12 Nautilus exercises in less than 25 minutes. As you work yourself into better condition, the time between exercises should be reduced. It is entirely possible to go through a workout of 12 Nautilus exercises in less than 15 minutes. Such a workout not only develops muscular size and strength but also develops a high level of cardiovascular endurance.

MORE IS NOT BETTER

An advanced trainee does not need more Nautilus exercise than a beginner; rather, the need changes in the direction of *harder but less.*

Beginning trainees usually show acceptable strength gains on most types of exercise programs, even though they may perform several sets of more than 12 repetitions in each training session. They are able to make this progress, at least for a while, because they are not strong enough to use up all their recovery ability. As they get stronger, however, they do use that recovery ability, and their progress stops. The stronger the individual becomes, the greater resistance he handles and the greater inroads he makes into his recovery ability. So advanced trainees must reduce their overall Nautilus exercises from 12 to 10 and train at high intensity only twice a week. On Monday they might train hard, on Wednesday less strenuously, and on Friday hard again. The Wednesday workout would not stimulate growth, but it would keep the trainee's muscles from atrophying. It would permit growth by not making significant inroads into the athlete's recovery ability.

SEQUENCE

Workouts should begin with the largest muscle groups and proceed to the smallest. This is important for two reasons: working the largest muscles first causes the greatest degree of overall body stimulation; and it is impossible to reach momentary muscular exhaustion in a large muscle if the smaller muscle group serving as a link between the resistance and the large muscle groups has already been exhausted. Thus it is important to work the largest muscles first while the system is still capable of working with the desired intensity.

For best results, the exercise sequence should be as follows:

1. Hips
2. Legs
3. Torso
4. Arms
5. Waist
6. Lower back
7. Neck

VARIETY

The human body quickly grows accustomed to almost any kind of activity. Once this happens, no amount of participation in the same activity will provide growth stimulation. It is, therefore, important to provide many forms of variation in Nautilus training. Variation can be made in several different ways. Weight or repetitions can be varied for each workout. The exercises can be changed occasionally, alternated, or performed in a different sequence. And training days can be varied.

FREQUENCY

Between Nautilus workouts you should rest at least 48 hours but not more than 96 hours.

High-intensity Nautilus exercise causes a complex chemical reaction inside a muscle. If given time, the muscle will compensate by causing certain cells to get bigger and stronger. High-intensity exercise is, therefore, necessary to stimulate muscular growth. But it is not the only requirement. The stimulated muscle must be given time to grow.

Research performed at Ohio State University by Drs. Edward Fox and Robert Bartels has shown that there should be approximately 48 hours between workouts, but 72–96 hours between sessions are required for extremely strong athletes. High levels of muscular size and strength begin to decrease and atrophy after 96 hours of normal activity. This means that you should exercise every other day.

An every-other-day, three-times-per-week Nautilus program also seems to provide the body with the needed irregularity of training. A first workout is performed on Monday. Two days later, a second workout is performed on Wednesday and a third on Friday. On Sunday the system is expecting and is prepared for a fourth workout, but it does not come. Instead, it comes a day later—on Monday, when the body is neither expecting nor prepared for it. This schedule of training prevents the body from falling into a regular routine. Since the system is never quite able to adjust to this irregularity of training, growth is stimulated.

SUPERVISION

Perhaps some individuals can push themselves to a 100-

percent effort occasionally, or on two or three Nautilus exercises, but experience proves that this is virtually impossible to do consistently.

Nautilus high-intensity exercise is not easy. Properly performed, it is very demanding, and it is not surprising that few people can do it on their own initiative. An instructor is needed to supervise and urge most trainees to work at the required level of intensity.

An example from running should help clarify this concept:

An athlete can run a quarter-mile in 50 seconds by applying 100-percent effort. His pain during the last 100 yards will be almost unbearable. He rationalizes, therefore, that if he slows slightly to run the distance in 55 seconds, he will probably get 90-percent results. If he repeats the 55-second quarter-mile three times, he falsely reasons that he will accomplish more than by running the track one time with 100-percent effort.

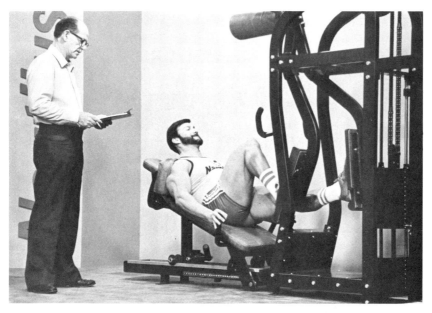

Arthur Jones supervises Boyer Coe on the duo squat machine. It is impossible to overestimate the importance of quality supervision. (Photo by Ellington Darden)

But he will never get the degree of results from running 55-second quarter-miles three times that he would have by running the track with one 100-percent effort. It is the 100-percent effort that forces his body to overcompensate and get stronger. Ninety-percent efforts, regardless of how many times they are repeated, will never approach the results attained by one 100-percent effort.

The same applies to building strength. If you can do 11 repetitions in a stringent effort on a given Nautilus exercise but instead stop at 10, you have not reached your potential.

This is why supervision is all-important. You cannot push yourself hard enough. You need a supervisor to tell you when to slow down, to hold your head back, and to relax your lower body when working your upper body. You must be reminded to eliminate excessive gripping and facial expressions, to do the last repetition of each exercise, and to perform numerous other activities that make each Nautilus exercise harder and more productive.

KEEPING ACCURATE RECORDS

You should keep accurate records of workout-by-workout progress. This can be done on a card that lists the exercises with ample space to the right for recording the date, resistance, repetitions, and training time.

WARMING UP AND COOLING DOWN

Warming up may be, as some authorities believe, more psychological than physiological. But there is ample evidence to support the case for warming up as a safeguard against injury. During the warm-up the cartilages of the knee increase their thickness and provide a better fit of the surfaces of the knee joint. Frictionlike resistance of the muscle cells is reduced by the higher temperature of the body, and the elasticity of the tendons and ligaments is increased. The change to higher temperature not only augments speed of movement and power potential but also minimizes risk of injury.

A rise in temperature of the muscle cells by only a few degrees speeds up the production of energy by one-third. These changes in the human mechanism are similar to those that occur in an automobile as it warms up.

Almost any sequence of light calisthenic movements can be used as a general warm-up to precede a vigorous Nautilus training session. Suggested movements include head rotation, side bend, trunk twist, squat, and stationary cycling. Doing each movement for a minute or so will be sufficient. Specific warming up for each body part occurs during the first four repetitions of each Nautilus exercise.

Cooling down after your workout is also important. This prevents blood from pooling in your exercised muscles. After your last exercise, cool down by walking around the workout area, getting a drink of water, and moving your arms in slow circles. Continue these easy movements for four or five minutes or until your breathing has returned to normal and your heart rate has slowed.

NAUTILUS TRAINING FOR WOMEN

Many women believe that, if they participate in Nautilus exercise, they will become large and unfeminine in appearance. But it is virtually impossible for a woman to develop excessively large muscles.

Building large muscles requires two factors. First, the individual must have long muscle bellies and short tendon attachments. Second, an adequate amount of male hormones, particularly testosterone, must be present in the bloodstream. Women seldom have long muscle bellies; in fact, it is even rare among men. And women have less than one-hundredth the amount of testosterone in their blood as do men.

Before puberty there is little difference between the muscular size and strength of boys and that of girls. Once puberty begins, testosterone from the male testes and estrogen from the female ovaries enter the bloodstream, triggering the development of the appropriate secondary sexual characteristics.

A small percentage of women do have large muscles, particularly in their legs, which in most cases may be inherited or the result of an above-average amount of testosterone in the system. The adrenal glands and the sex glands in both men and women secrete a small amount of the nondominant hormone. If a larger-than-usual amount of testosterone is secreted in a female, she has the potential for greater muscle development. There are also men who have an above-average amount of estrogen in their systems, which tends to give them a feminine appearance.

Generally speaking, 99.99 percent of American women could not develop large muscles under any circumstances. But Nautilus exercise is worthwhile because it strengthens and conditions their muscles and prevents injuries.

12 RULES FOR NAUTILUS TRAINING

1. Perform one set of 4–6 exercises for the lower body and 6–8 exercises for the upper body, and not more than 12 exercises in any workout.

2. Select a resistance for each exercise that allows you to do between 8 and 12 repetitions.

3. Continue each exercise until no additional repetitions are possible. When 12 or more repetitions are performed, increase the resistance by approximately 5 percent at the next workout.

4. Work the largest muscles first and move quickly from one exercise to the next. This procedure develops cardiovascular endurance.

5. Concentrate on flexibility by slowly stretching during the first three repetitions of each exercise.

6. Accentuate the lowering portion of each repetition.

7. Move slower, never faster, if in doubt about the speed of movement.

8. Do everything possible to isolate and work each large muscle group to exhaustion.

9. Attempt constantly to increase the number of repetitions or the amount of weight or both. But do not sacrifice form in an attempt to produce results.

10. Train no more than three times a week.

11. Keep accurate records—date, resistance, repetitions, and overall training time—of each workout.

12. Vary the workouts.

Do not split a Nautilus routine into upper body one day and lower body the next. Both the upper and lower body should be trained in the same workout. Results will be better if you train your lower body before your upper body.

WORDS OF CAUTION

Before beginning a Nautilus training program, you should undergo a medical examination. Vigorous exercise can be dangerous for some people. Intense physical activity coupled with certain environmental conditions may aggravate existing asthmatic conditions. People with a tendency toward high blood pressure should be supervised closely in any heavy lifting or straining exercises that may cause temporary increases in that pressure. Those over the age of 35, and coronary-prone younger people who possess high-risk factors, should obtain a stress-test electrocardiogram. Stress tests are particularly important to those who have the following risk factors: overweight, hypertension, diabetes, sedentary lifestyle, cigarette smoking, and a family history of early heart disease.

8

Super-Slow Training

How would you like to get over 50 percent better strength-training results from your Nautilus training?

Well, it's possible if you apply the super-slow protocol to each Nautilus machine.

The super-slow protocol requires a positive contraction of 10 seconds and a negative contraction of 4 seconds.

Before we examine the reasoning behind this very slow method of training, the results of two recent studies that I completed will be of interest to you.

SUPER-SLOW RESEARCH

In 1985 I supervised the training of 65 women between the ages of 19 and 64. The standard Nautilus principles, as described in Chapter 7, were used to train these women three times a week for 10 consecutive weeks. Lower body strength and upper body strength were measured on all women before and after the 10-week training period.

Lower body strength was tested on the leg extension machine, and the maximum weight that could be performed for 10 repetitions was recorded. Upper body strength was measured in a similar manner on the pullover machine. Overall strength gained was determined by adding together the 10-repetition maximums on the leg extension and the pullover and then dividing by two. Percent strength increase was calculated by subtracting the *before* average from the *after* average and then dividing this by the *before* average.

The average overall strength gain in 10 weeks was 30.4 percent, or 3.04 percent per week.

In the fall of 1986 and the summer of 1987 I supervised a similar group of 49 women. They all adhered to the same basic Nautilus principles as the first group, with two major changes. One, the study lasted only 6 weeks, as opposed to 10 weeks. Two, the women performed each Nautilus machine in a super-slow manner—10 seconds up and 4 seconds down—as opposed to 2 seconds up and 4 seconds down.

The results for the super-slow group were surprising. The average woman improved her overall strength 28.94 percent. But remember, the duration of the study was 6 weeks, rather than 10 weeks. Thus, the average strength increase per week was 4.83 percent.

The 4.83 percent increase per week for the super-slow group, versus the 3.04 percent increase for the standard group, represents a 59 percent improvement in favor of the super-slow group. Essentially, the super-slow group got the same results in 6 weeks as the standard training group received in 10 weeks.

THE EFFECTIVENESS OF SUPER-SLOW

Super-slow training is effective because it eliminates momentum. Momentum in an exercise occurs when you perform fast, jerky repetitions.

If you start with a quick jerk, then the moving weight can actually pull your body along for the ride, until you have to catch the weight, which is now stopped, in the top position. Such fast, jerky lifting contributes to disproportionate, unbalanced strength development. It neglects many muscle fibers and overstresses others. And it is dangerous and can cause injuries.

Slow, smooth, deliberate repetitions, on the other hand, involve a maximum number of muscle fibers. Involving a maximum number of muscle fibers more thoroughly is a key to effectiveness. Furthermore, super-slow repetitions are much safer than other methods of training.

THE SAFETY FACTOR

"Safety was our primary concern," said Ken Hutchins, who Nautilus-trained more than 200 older women involved in a special osteoporosis project at the University of Florida. "Most older women do not have the motor coordination to move safely against resistance—unless it is performed very slowly. In fact, osteoporotics can actually crush their own bones if they practice much in the way of slamming and banging of weights."

Ken and his co-worker, Brenda Hutchins, spent months in tedious trial-and-error comparative training until they finally were confident of the protocol. "Every time a trainee moved slower on the positive phase of a repetition," Ken noted, "given that the movement never actually stopped, the trainee produced better results." Of course, slower exercising also requires better instruction, better concentration, and better communication between the trainer and the trainee. Such quality interactions are already in short supply in most fitness centers.

Ken Hutchins is the person most responsible for developing the basic guidelines for super-slow training. In fact, he has published a 150-page manual entitled *The Ultimate Exercise Protocol: Super Slow,* which is listed in the bibliography. Let's examine the guidelines in more detail.

BASIC GUIDELINES

Super-slow training on Nautilus equipment applies a positive contraction of 10 seconds and a negative contraction of 4 seconds. In other words, lift the weight in approximately 10 seconds, then lower it to the beginning position in 4 seconds.

At the beginning, you should use a helper with a stopwatch to count the time on each repetition. Ask yourself how slowly you can move without stopping. Let's consider this in two different Nautilus machines, the leg extension and the pullover.

Performing the Leg Extension

Sit in the proper position with your ankles behind the roller pads. Try to just break the weight stack—barely start to move the resistance. You may move it only a perceptible ⅛ inch. The less you move it, the more control you demonstrate.

Once you've started, slow down. Continue to straighten the legs and arrive at the fully extended position at about the 10-second mark.

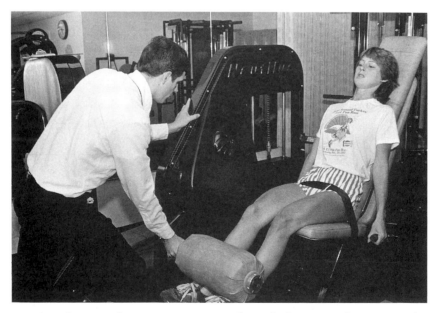

Ken Hutchins coaches a young woman through the super-slow protocol on the leg extension machine.

If you do not precisely hit 10 seconds, do not be overly concerned. Just aim for 10. Any duration between 8 and 12 seconds is acceptable, but aim for 10. Do not suddenly speed up at the end of the movement merely because you believe your movement is too slow.

Deliberately pause in the contracted position. Then ease out of it gradually. Smoothly increase speed, but still move slowly, and return to the starting position in about 4 seconds.

Feel the weight stack touch, but do not let the slack out of the chain or rest. You want to touch, then barely move again in the positive direction. Start the next repetition immediately but slowly.

Once the resistance becomes difficult, you will tend to alternately stop and heave into the resistance. Try to avoid this. Keep the movement arm traveling at a near constant speed. When it appears that further movement is impossible without compromise of form, failure is attained.

Judge resistance increases with the stopwatch. Once a set begins, start the clock. Stop the clock when movement halts or cheating techniques become evident.

The selected resistance should permit you to perform an exercise for at least 60 seconds. This generally works out to be about four repetitions.

Once you can perform over 100 seconds (seven to eight repetitions) without compromising form, a resistance increase is indicated for the next workout.

Performing the Pullover

Enter the machine in the usual fashion. Allow the movement arm to pull your shoulders into a stretched position. This is the beginning of the exercise. Start the stopwatch here.

Squeeze the elbows against the upholstery. Steadily increase the force until movement occurs. Proceed very slowly. Do not allow momentum to develop at any point along the range. The entire positive movement should require about 10 seconds.

With a stopwatch in hand, Brenda Hutchins monitors the slowness of the positive movement as a subject performs a pullover. Remember, in a super-slow repetition, the positive work takes 10 seconds and the negative work requires 4 seconds.

Pause in the contracted position. Then ease out of the contracted position, slightly increasing the speed. Maintain smoothness. As the stretch is again encountered, move cautiously. Stretch slowly. This, the negative phase of the exercise, should require about four seconds.

Begin the next repetition.

Using the standard protocol, the first 15–30 degrees of movement occur quickly. This is common even though the average velocity of the entire movement is acceptably slow.

Almost all of this momentum can be eliminated from such an exercise, but this requires a little practice. You must develop a feel for how fast you move off the mark. The following mental picture may help.

Mental Practice

Sit in the pullover machine. Assume the stretched position. Pretend that the required force to move the movement arm is 100 pounds. With no intention to move, start to pull slightly with the involved muscles. Pretend that your muscles are pulling with only five pounds of force. Nothing happens. No movement occurs.

Increase the force to 10 pounds, then 20, then 30, then 50, then 75, then 90, then 100. Still, no movement occurs.

Then apply 101 pounds of force. The machine begins to move. Until now, the pads have compressed, and the body has slightly contorted, but no movement of the machine has occurred.

But with 101 pounds of force, slight acceleration occurs and the machine moves.

Of course, this entire mental picture is applied in a time frame of approximately a second. The essence of the idea is a gradual buildup of force, as opposed to a sudden one.

Have you ever waited at a rail crossing while a long train stopped and then proceeded? Do you remember the characteristic clatter that moved down the full length of the train as it started? And did you notice that the caboose started to move forward long after the engine was already in motion?

There is a certain amount of unavoidable play in the coupling arms on each train car. If the couplers are pulling, this play is totally eliminated. If they are pushing, the play is as wide as it can be.

When the train stops, the play often widens. Then, as it starts, the play is removed. That loud clatter is the result of a tremendous force imparted to each successive coupler as the train accelerates forward. Acceleration of the train generally occurs very smoothly and slowly. On close inspection, this slow, smooth acceleration is actually a series of sudden and violent accelerations.

The play in each coupler represents slack in the system between the front and rear ends of the train. The caboose will begin to move forward only after all of that slack is removed.

Pretend that your muscle-joint system is an accelerating train. And pretend that you are going to accelerate your train in such a fashion that the couplers make no noise. To do this you must start each repetition of an exercise ever so gradually. Consider this concept as you begin the positive phase of each repetition of an exercise. You will provide more exercise to that part of the muscle's function, and forces will be minimized even further.

Understanding Friction

Ken and Brenda Hutchins directed the exercise for the Nautilus-funded osteoporosis research from 1982–1986. At first, they failed to elicit smooth and controlled movements from their female research subjects using the standard Nautilus protocol: lift the resistance in 2 seconds, lower it in 4 seconds. They then resorted to a very slow protocol that they had experimented with in 1981. Using the guideline to lift the resistance in 10 seconds, and lower it in 4 seconds, they succeeded with the required degree of control and safety that they needed for their research. They called this style the *super-slow protocol.*

Applying super slow required some new guidelines and techniques. It also forced Ken and Brenda to recognize requirements in exercise that should be obvious, but were never considered before. The most important observation was the need for friction-free exercise equipment.

Super-slow protocol was applied, in part, to eliminate excessive momentum from exercise. Friction inherent in an exercise machine increases as the device slows or stops movement. In other words, Nautilus machines used with the super-slow protocol tended to hangup—break free—hangup—break free, resulting in less than acceptably smooth movement. Ken and Brenda then realized that exercise required equipment with no perceivable friction.

Later, Ken realized that the ultimate efficiency of the Nautilus cam was at stake. Its effectiveness was hampered significantly by friction. Removing friction with the application of bearings would result in exercise efficiency never before experienced.

Exercise efficiency depends on maintenance of a meaningful levered load against skeletal muscle. The muscle must remain loaded during all phases of the exercise movement. Momentum can effectively unload muscle. So can friction.

There are two sources of friction in exercise. *Bodily friction* is that friction in your muscles and joints. It has long been recognized to approximate a magnitude of 20 percent and is not improvable. *Machine friction* is that friction in the exercise device and it can be reduced to less than 1 percent with the application of bearings. There is no such thing as zero friction, but if friction is so low as to be imperceptible, then it is effectively zero. *System friction* is used to describe the sum of machine friction plus bodily friction.

Example: Ignore strength and resistance variation and pretend that you can produce exactly 130 pounds of force with your biceps throughout a curling movement. Also ignore bodily friction for the sake of discussion.

If the machine friction equals 30 percent, you can lift 100 pounds plus 30 percent friction. One hundred pounds plus 30 percent friction equal 130 pounds produced by your body. You produce 130 pounds of force to lift 100 pounds plus friction. The device provides you with a total of 130 pounds of resistance as you lift it, but how much resistance is provided when you lower it? The answer is 70 pounds: 100 pounds minus 30 percent. The load varies 85.7 percent from negative (70) to positive (130) phase.

Looking at this in reverse, the load varies 46 percent from the positive (130) to the negative (70). Your muscle is un-loaded 46 percent on the negative with an inherent 30 percent friction.

If we reduce the machine friction to 1 percent, you can lift 128.71 pounds on the machine. Your actual total resistance is still 130: 128.71 plus 1 percent friction equal 130. You could then lower 131.28 pounds, but since 2.56 pounds are not added to the weight stack to make up for the friction you actually experience 127.43 pounds (130 minus 127.43 divided by 130 equals 1.9 percent). Your muscles are unloaded 1.9 percent.

If we compare the unloading that occurred between the machine with 30 percent friction versus 1 percent, we see unloading during the negative phase reduced from 46 percent to 1.9 percent. When we appreciate that muscle recovers very quickly and that partial and brief unloading can dramatically reduce exercise efficiency, then we realize that friction reduc-tion potentiates a quantum leap in this efficiency.

Nautilus now manufactures a growing line of *low-friction* exercise machines. Ken Hutchins's prediction was correct. With the appropriate resistance, the first few repetitions feel too light. Quickly, it seems correct, then suddenly almost impossible, then soon as if someone added resistance to the weight stack. This is merely an illusion due to the reduction of friction in the new Nautilus equipment.

SELECTING THE RESISTANCE

In super-slow training, you will need less resistance as compared to the resistance that you normally handle for 8–12 repetitions. A good guideline to follow is to reduce the weight on the machine that you normally use by approximately 30 percent. This deliberately underestimates the resistance that you probably need, but it allows you to begin with very strict form. Increase the resistance in each exercise gradually until perfect form permits 60–100 seconds of work.

Super-slow training can be applied to all Nautilus exercises, even those that involve compound movements. Care must be taken in compound movements, however, to avoid or minimize the time spent in a position of infinite moment arm. This is a position where an extremity's bones are aligned so that effective resistance is zero. It is a common problem encountered in exercises such as a chin-up or pulldown.

For example: Start the pulldown movement by slightly bending the arms. If you are not careful, you will move the first few degrees so suddenly that your extended arms encounter no real work. Then, on the return, go all the way to the straight position. But move immediately and slowly out of this position. If you linger in this spot, the intensity of the exercise is compromised.

NEGATIVE WORK AND SLOW TRAINING

The basic Nautilus principles suggest that the negative portion of a Nautilus exercise be performed twice as slowly as the lifting phase. You may be wondering why the negative phase of the super-slow approach remains at 4 seconds, as opposed to 2 times 10, or 20 seconds.

Since super-slow training requires such slow movement, the resistance levels are reduced significantly. The quality of the back pressure involved during the lowering portion of the exercise is also reduced. If you move slower than a rate of 4 seconds, negative work during this phase is reduced even further because of your ability to rest partially. In other words, going slower means easier—exactly opposite of our intensity requirements.

Also, simply dropping the resistance makes the work easier. Therefore, keep the rate of movement during the lowering phase the same as the standard protocol.

Because slow training requires a positive movement of 10 seconds and a negative movement of 4 seconds, many trainees might assume that negative work is less important than positive work. But this is not the case. Negative work is just as important in slow training as in normal training. Indeed, it is even more important.

Without the back pressure of negative work, you would be able to move positively, then rest, then continue positively again. Negative work potential is crucially important during the lifting portion of super-slow training. It is invaluable for maintaining high-intensity work.

ADVANTAGES OF SLOW TRAINING

Super-slow training serves as the best means to correct poor form in any exercise involving positive contraction. It eliminates momentum, serves to isolate those glossed-over points in your range of motion where you habitually and otherwise undetectably shift, shrug, lunge, heave, and invoke other muscles to complete the movement. These weak areas are better addressed, since you are more aware of each position of possible motion and reliance on momentum is restricted. For the same reasons, the exercise is safer because of lowered forces.

Most importantly, super-slow training—because of the thoroughness of its muscular involvement—produces better strength-training results from Nautilus exercise.

DISADVANTAGES OF SLOW TRAINING

Super-slow exercise may be boring to some. Also, the intensity of contraction may prove to be too uncomfortable.

It's not an easy or fun way to train. Exercise is most efficient, however, when it is most difficult and least fun. Super-slow exercise is very effective and beneficially so. And tangible benefits often serve to motivate the most discouraged trainee.

Slow training may prove cumbersome in a commercial facility. Done well, it often requires an instructor with a stopwatch. But with a little practice, the stopwatch can be discarded. The repetition scheme already outlined will suffice.

GREAT FOR OLDER WOMEN, GREAT FOR BODYBUILDING

Super-slow training is tailor-made for older women because it is safe and effective. It may be even more beneficial for bodybuilding because it allows you to isolate a muscle group better than normal training does. Effective muscle isolation leads to better and more complete development.

Initially, you should experiment with super-slow training during several workouts. It will take at least three sessions to learn the skill of moving slowly on each repetition. Once you have mastered the skill, there are three basic ways that you can use super-slow training.

One, use it on all of your exercises as a change of pace for two weeks in a row. Then go back to your normal workout for the next three months and try it again.

Two, use it selectively on Nautilus machines that you have reached a plateau on. For example, suppose you've been stuck on the leg curl with 120 pounds for the last month. You cannot do more than 10 repetitions in the normal fashion with that weight. So, you reduce the resistance and try super-slow leg curls for three consecutive training sessions. That should promptly help you to break out of your training slump on the leg curl. You should now be able to perform at least 12 repetitions with 120 pounds. The same concept can be applied to any Nautilus machine.

Three, use it for all of your Nautilus workouts.

9

Cardiovascular Fitness

One major focus of today's interest in exercise is cardiovascular fitness. The promotion of such fitness is appropriate. A value judgment, however, may be involved.

If jogging three miles daily for 20 years increases the expected life span from 70 to 72 years, would it be worthwhile? Most Americans would probably answer, "No."

But if a 20-minute exercise routine practiced three times per week for 20 years increases the expected life span by 2 years and enables a more active and productive life, would it be worthwhile? Most Americans would probably answer, "Yes."

Cardiovascular diseases, pulmonary insufficiencies, and disorders of the muscles and bones appear to be somewhat linked. Collectively these disorders cost our country trillions of dollars in care for pain and loss of productivity. They can all be lessened in incidence and severity.

Many believe that the best hedge against future health

problems is jogging. If jogging is not appropriate, then other so-called "aerobic" activities are to be sought—such as swimming, bicycling, dancing, and racquet sports.

What is *aerobic*?

Aerobic generally refers to an activity that involves an increased participation of the heart and lungs for a prolonged time period. If the heart rate doubles when you run across a busy intersection and then returns to normal after a few seconds or minutes, the activity is generally said to be *anaerobic, or not* aerobic. If the activity is continued long enough at an adequate pace to sustain an elevated heart rate for many minutes, then it is said to be *aerobic*.

Specifically, *aerobic* refers to the aerobic metabolic pathways. Biochemists recognize different elements of the Kreb's Citric Acid Cycle as requiring free oxygen from the bloodstream for aerobic metabolism to work. Anaerobic metabolic pathways require oxygen but not free oxygen.

AEROBIC AND ANAEROBIC ACTIVITY

The only practical guideline for measuring the aerobic effect of an activity is sustained heart rate elevation. There are charts showing target zones. These estimate the beneficial heart rate according to age and sex. Generally, the charts recommend that people exercise hard enough to elevate their heart rates to from 70 to 85 percent of their maximum heart rate. The target zones are the reflection of a bell-shaped curve spread over many tested individuals. The zones therefore do not show the requirements for those 4 or 5 individuals out of 100 who fall into the extreme upper and lower ends of the curve.

Some of the highest sustained heart rates recorded during exercise were demonstrated during the West Point Study conducted by Nautilus Sports/Medical Industries. During the first workout the heart rates of all of the 19 trainees were sustained between 205 and 228 beats per minute for 30–40 minutes. Although the work performed per minute was increased by 60 percent during the following 16 workouts, the heart rate during the last workout remained between 170 and 190. One man exceeded 190.

Recently, heart rate elevation has been criticized as not necessarily indicative of aerobic work. Critics claim that elevated heart rate and labored breathing may occur even when the aerobic metabolic pathways are not taxed. Some claim that continuous steady-state activities must be employed to truly tax the intended pathways. What we witness is a dichotomy between the general and the specific definition of *aerobic.*

What does this argument mean? Why is there disagreement on the subject of aerobic fitness?

Keith Johnson, MD, of the University of Florida, explains the confusion quite simply. His first point of criticism is the traditional concept of threshold—aerobic and anaerobic threshold. "These concepts are convenient teaching tools for students," Dr. Johnson says, "but become ingrained as underserved realities. There is no sharp threshold or demarcation between the body's metabolic pathways as the terms imply. Both systems work continuously in all activities. Research has not shown whether the aerobic and anaerobic systems change proportionately with different activity levels, or both increase with a genetically dictated and virtually constant ratio."

STEADY-STATE ACTIVITY AND CIRCUIT TRAINING

Steady state is usually defined as a perpetual motion activity, where the same act is continued for long periods. Jogging, bicycling, walking, swimming, and some sports activities qualify as steady state.

Steady state is inappropriately defined in this manner, and this leads to confusion. Rather than referring to steady state as perpetual activity, the more useful concept of steady state is *perpetual muscular work.*

Circuit training denotes different activities or exercises performed in tandem.

Some exercise physiologists argue that steady-state activities are superior to circuit training for the purpose of cardiovascular fitness. This is naturally believed, since circuit training is rarely performed correctly with proper attention to detail and planning. Rest often occurs between the exercises, and thus the heart rate is not adequately sustained to promote the fitness desired.

Properly conducted Nautilus training, performed in a circuit fashion, is steady-state muscular work for much of the core, torso musculature. These muscles are required for stabilization during all exercise. The abdominal and erector spinae muscles, for instance, are almost impossible to isolate out of exercises intended for the extremities. They work continuously if no rest is allowed between exercises.

The lack of understanding that surrounds the concept of steady state justifies skepticism, unless its use is well defined. This is the watchword when any serious literature search is performed. Physiologists rarely consider circuit training to be steady state in a muscular sense. Nevertheless, it is steady state when properly performed.

TREADMILLS OF OUR MINDS

A second criticism advanced by Dr. Keith Johnson exposes the problem of cardiovascular testing. Such testing takes the form of either an EKG maximum stress test or a maximum oxygen uptake test. Both are traditionally performed on a treadmill.

Dr. Johnson submits that there is little wonder that jogging and running are so praised for their cardiovascular benefit. Testing is performed on treadmills, and the act of running becomes the popular fixation.

It is extremely difficult to test maximum oxygen uptake during circuit training. This is being attempted by some, though the logistics of moving the testing equipment while maintaining calibrations and preventing hose leaks is formidable as the subject moves quickly from station to station.

Some believe that the treadmill-performed test is a valid indicator of cardiovascular improvements. This, however, is an oversimplification.

Dr. Keith Johnson tests a middle-aged woman's ability to consume oxygen while walking on a motor-driven treadmill. It is easier to measure oxygen uptake if the person is walking rather than running. But even vigorous running on a treadmill, combined with oxygen uptake, is easier to measure than trying to measure accurately oxygen consumption during a Nautilus workout. This is one reason why there is so much confusion in the area of strength training and cardiovascular endurance. (Photo by Ken Hutchins.)

THE FUNCTION OF THE HEART AND LUNGS

Consider the function of the heart and lungs. They simply deliver nutrients and oxygen to working muscles and export waste from them. But, again, the muscles are the key.

Research shows that conventional exercise devices—barbells and similar tools—are about 6–10 percent efficient. This figure represents those parts of the muscle fibers that reach failure when exercise can no longer be continued. Six to 10 percent is quite high. But it assumes that the exercises are performed correctly. As usually perfomed—that is, in a haphazard manner—these exercises are less efficient.

Traditional steady-state activities, such as jogging and cycling, bring only about 1 percent of the muscle fibers to failure. This explains why the activity can be continued. Though inefficient, steady-state exercises can and do tax enough muscle throughout the body to cause a sustained and elevated heart rate.

But this effect does not compare with what is possible when the large muscles of the body are taxed 6–10 percent with the proper use of a barbell. The exercises are multiple-joint movements and are not steady state in the sense of a single, continued activity. But the heart and lungs don't know or care about this. They only *know* that a tremendous transport demand is being asked of them. They are behind in their work, and before they can catch up to the demand imposed by the first exercise the subject is starting the third or fourth. Again, part of the musculature is worked continuously. That musculature, worked in tandem, is worked at 10 times the efficiency encountered during the traditional steady-state activities. Of course, a greater effect is achieved with Nautilus equipment.

It is possible to run or jog with no cardiovascular benefit. It is possible to strength-train with no cardiovascular benefit. Properly performed, Nautilus training will provide benefits to cardiovascular fitness in a few months that no amount of traditional aerobic or steady-state exercise can approach after years of training. These statements are based on empirical observation and logic, not necessarily on formalized research.

WHAT RESEARCH SHOWS

During Nautilus seminars the question is often asked, "How does strength training contribute to cardiovascular endurance?" Dr. Keith Johnson answers:

> Remember that cardiovascular endurance is only one of the five main aspects of physical fitness, others being muscular strength, joint flexibility, body leanness, and reduced risk of injury. Although some activities emphasize one aspect more than others, all five are important.

Cardiovascular fitness means different things to different people. To the medical community it refers to one's probability of not suffering a heart attack. To the athletic community it refers to one's probability of performing well at an endurance event. But it's hard to measure probability in a laboratory. Therefore, the scientific community has chosen something they can measure, *maximal oxygen uptake* or *aerobic capacity*. They have defined cardiovascular endurance as "the body's ability to absorb, transport, and utilize oxygen."

Just as genetic potential limits our ultimate strength, so does it limit our ultimate endurance. To discover the primary factor limiting maximal oxygen uptake, let's review the oxygen pathways, from absorption in the lungs and transport through the circulatory system to consumption by the muscle.

Panting joggers would agree, if they could just get more air, they could be more enduring. This, however, is not the case. The purpose of the lungs is to saturate the blood with oxygen, and they do this quite easily under nearly all conditions, including maximal exercise. In fact, the lungs have been blessed with a generous reserve. At rest, total saturation of the blood traveling through the capillaries in the lungs occurs within the first one-third of the total transit time. During maximal exercise the heart rate and blood flow increase, thereby reducing the transit time by one-half. This still is enough time for all of the blood entering the lungs to become totally saturated with oxygen.

In the short time that it takes blood to flow through the capillaries in a working muscle all of the available oxygen is consumed. Hence, both the lungs and muscle are loading and unloading oxygen at nearly 100 percent efficiency and are not the limiting factor in oxygen uptake.

The circulatory system, however, does not measure up quite so well. The purpose of the heart is to pump oxygenated blood to the rest of the body. If we look at how much blood the heart can pump compared to the amount of oxygen the body consumes, we find a direct one-to-one correlation. That is, if the heart could pump more blood, the body could consume more oxygen. This relationship had led many physiologists to conclude that the heart is the limiting factor in oxygen uptake and that endurance exercise trains the heart to pump more effectively.

Other physiologists disagree. They conclude that, since the heart can pump out only as much blood as returns to it, the peripheral vasculature must be the bottleneck. It resists every attempt by the heart to increase blood flow. But how does exercise affect this resistance?

During exercise, when a muscle contracts, the pressure within that muscle rises, compressing the blood vessels, restricting its own blood flow. Studies have shown that when a muscle contracts at less than 20 percent of its maximal voluntary contraction, there is no restriction to blood flow. Contractions of greater intensity, however, do compromise flow. With contractions at 50–60 percent of maximum, there is no flow whatsoever. Without blood flow there is no oxygen delivery and no oxygen consumption.

There are two ways to decrease the intensity of muscular contractions during an activity. The first is to become more *skillful* at that activity, thereby wasting less effort. The other is to become *stronger,* so it requires a smaller percentage of the available muscle mass.

Whereas skill is highly specific, strength is applicable to any situation. An endurance runner can also become an endurance swimmer by learning efficient swimming technique. But he can improve in both activities by making his muscles stronger.

As genetic potential ultimately limits how strong we can be, so does strength ultimately limit how enduring we can be.

10

More on Cardiovascular Fitness

"People aren't dying from lack of muscular strength," says Dr. Jack Wilmore, a professor of physical education at the University of Texas who was recently quoted in the *Wall Street Journal.* "They're dying from heart disease."

The above concept is commonly heard from exercise physiologists all over this country, as well as from physicians and nurses. Their logic is correct, but their premise is unsound. Their conclusion, therefore, is probably wrong.

The most common cause of death noted on death certificates in the United States is cardiovascular insufficiency. This is especially prevalent among age-related deaths. It is true that the vascular system is usually the vital organ that ultimately fails. And this misleads us.

The real cause of death among the elderly is immobility. Once the bones and joints and muscles are so debilitated that

Dr. Michael Fulton, of Daytona Beach, Florida, explains the importance of skeletal muscle strengthening and its positive effects on cardiovascular endurance and bone density.

movement becomes impossible, eventual cardiovascular insufficiency leads to death.

Immobility refers to inability to move. It does not necessarily refer to inactivity.

The Spine and Sports Rehabilitation Clinic of Daytona Beach, Florida, is currently researching the treatment of paraplegia with Nautilus training. With the assistance of several neurologists, Dr. Michael Fulton hopes to stimulate high-intensity muscular contractions. The goal of this approach is to promote vascular and bony integrity through muscular work. These patients commonly die at an early adult age due to osteoporosis and vascular insufficiencies. They are immobile for many practical purposes, especially their lower bodies.

Many of the degenerative diseases of the aging process appear to be interrelated. This idea does not surprise most histologists. They often point out that crystals that are lost from the bone latticework in the process of osteoporosis also appear to be the culprits in arteriosclerotic plaque formation.

And there appears to be a logical relationship between the strength of muscle and bone.

Elderly subjects often present a greatly diminished cardiovascular response to Nautilus training at the outset. They are so weak and possess so little muscle that their response is slight when their muscles are isolated. Cardiovascular taxation does not appear to occur meaningfully until the following conditions are met.

1. Competency and confidence in the proper performance of the exercise are achieved.
2. The ability to contract the muscle intensely is learned.
3. Muscle mass is great enough to tax the support systems.

To meet these criteria, several months of strength training may be necessary. Until then, best results appear to come from a strength-training program coupled with a steady-state activity—preferably 20 minutes of bicycle ergometry three times weekly on identical days with the Nautilus workouts. As the trainee's condition improves, the results appear to get even better with the exclusion of the bicycle.

On the other hand, such a slow response graduation might be exactly what is indicated for advanced conditions of aging. In this sense, Nautilus is the ideal approach to exercise for the elderly. The best force control for the joints as well as the most gradual onset of cardiovascular response can be attained.

WALKING PROGRAMS

Few patients and few physicians understand what proper exercise is. They may never have experienced it. Physicians are at least aware that harm can result from those activities most often construed as exercise and do not want to be responsible for their patient's injuries.

But many patients expect an exercise prescription or recommendation from their personal physician. The physician feels compelled to say something. What can he say and still play it safe? What does he see as a harmless activity, immediately avail-able and convenient to everyone, requiring no special equip-ment, and no instructor? Walking. Walking is the doctor's cop-out.

Walking may indeed be indicated for a few individuals. And walking can produce physical benefits.

If a well-conditioned athlete spends most of his waking hours at a desk, taking a brisk walk in the night air will clear his mind. He will derive physical benefits, too. Walking will circulate some pooled blood, and his body will become warmer from increased muscular activity. If he does this once or so every other hour, he will feel better, think better, and perform better.

But will this or any walking program strengthen this athlete? No, it will not.

Walking does not provide productive exercise for most people. A few weakened individuals may slightly strengthen themselves from a walking program but only during the first few exposures.

Does walking promote cardiovascular fitness? It can for those individuals who are so debilitated that walking is de-manding. It remains a very poor stimulus to the average person with full mobility.

One 60-year-old woman put it very concisely. She lived across the street from a large nursing home where the elderly sit and rarely move all day. She said, "Yes, a walking program is great for them. It almost maintains their ability to walk."

Walking may indeed have a legitimate place as exercise, but there is often an extremely thin line between those rare unhealthy individuals who do find it meaningfully demanding and those who will be harmed by it.

As Dr. Keith Johnson points out, "The heart and lungs normally stay several steps ahead of the systems used to tax them." Osteoporotic deformities and debilities can reach a point where any movement to elevate the heart rate is precluded by the inability to move. The bones become so brittle due to disuse, hormone imbalances, calcium deficiencies, or all of the above that almost any force causes fractures.

The forces encountered during a brisk, even slow, walk are greater than most imagine. Some osteoporotic fractures occur simply from stepping off a curb or rotating the trunk while seated. An obvious accident, such as falling, is not necessary to cause such fractures.

Many people suffer sore feet, shinsplints, and backaches from prolonged standing. Prolonged walking certainly amplifies these forces, especially in the weakened musculatures of the elderly. Walking will induce little in the way of strengthening

Walking programs must be appraised according to the balance between benefit and risk. At the present time the benefits of walking are greatly exaggerated and the risks are largely unappreciated.

WOMEN AND AEROBIC DANCE

Attracting women to proper exercise has been one of the most difficult marketing problems ever tackled by commercial fitness clubs. Few commercial facilities or their women clients are currently aware that the key to a woman's improved cosmetic appeal is exercise that promotes muscle strengthening. For years, women were denied admission to strength-training areas.

When Vic Tanny, Sr., realized that strength training was the answer to women's figure problems, he spent several million dollars trying legitimately to attract them to his gyms. The year was 1953. Tanny's concepts attracted women for several years, especially in California and New York.

Other commercial facilities eventually built motorized equipment, vibrator belts, and other nonproductive passive exercise devices. These were marketed fairly successfully, but a feminized jargon was also necessary. In their spiel, the salesmen promised women improved "tone," "flexibility," and "firmness." Crucial to their advertising was the voluptuous woman in plush pink surroundings. These advertisements increased the membership flow with certain age groups. Still the masses were not interested.

Then, in 1980, along came aerobic dance. Many women were brought into the exercise world by the combined lure of movement that looked like fun and a group atmosphere that made them feel like they were all working together. Unfortunately, aerobic dancing is not the most efficient form of exercise for anyone, male or female.

Aerobic dancing does have an exercise effect, but it is slight. Primarily, it helps with cardiovascular fitness. Contrary to the belief of many people, it will do little to enhance muscular strength and endurance. If a woman chooses to perform aerobic dance for physical improvements, she will not derive all five of the definite physical benefits of exercise.

Compared to the physical results possible from partner-resisted movements or movements performed with broom

Aerobic dancing does *not* work all five components of physical fitness. It does nothing for flexibility, little for muscular strength, and can be dangerous. Properly performed, it can improve cardiovascular endurance and contribute to body leanness. (Photo by Ken Hutchins)

handles and milk jugs filled with water—in other words, strength-training regimens with the crudest of tools—dance is not as effective.

Aerobic dancing remains, however, the most efficient marketing tool for attracting women to a semblance of exercise. Furthermore, the marketing has overshot its goal in some cases. Some men are now attracted to dance, purportedly for reasons of exercise. A few college and professional football coaches now use and recommend it for conditioning athletes. Little do they realize that they are making a common and expected mistake. They violate the general principle of motor learning: specific skill practice.

Dance might help a football receiver if football were played on a stage and to music. The only way it would assist him skillwise is to improve his dancing ability in the end zone *after* a touchdown pass.

A COYOTE IN WINTER

Ken Hutchins, who developed the super-slow protocol, tells a story about a pet he had during his high school days in Conroe, Texas. His account has carry-over to aerobic conditioning:

> I once kept a tame coyote. He was a strange animal, especially in the presence of other dogs—very shy, cowering to everyone. His name was Karo.
>
> Karo hid most of the time or acted as though he was hiding from something. It was his nature. He liked the security of dark places—under the cattle guard, in culvert pipes, in abandoned fallout shelters, under the house. He was a pleasant-enough animal, but when I called him, I always expected to see him crawling out of or from under something.
>
> One winter I fiberglassed a canoe. I left a large pile of fabric remnants on the ground for about a week.
>
> After the first cold night I returned to check my work and found Karo crawling out from under the fiberglass to greet me.

He could not seem to bring himself to pay me much attention, though. His total preoccupation was scratching.

Karo had found not only another good hiding place but also warmth among my fiberglass remnants. What Karo didn't know was that, while fiberglass makes excellent insulation, it's also toxic to the skin. His time over the next several days included only two activities: scratching and staying warm.

The following week, Karo nearly froze to death. He had scratched off most of his hair and a great deal of skin. The poor dog never connected the scratching with the warmth of the fiberglass. And he certainly could not have fathomed the consequences.

Aerobic exercise enthusiasts are identical to Karo in some respects. They cannot begin to imagine the consequences of their present actions. They realize little how dangerous are the high forces they encounter during jogging or the long-range toll it will take on their bones and joints.

Likewise, dance aerobics participants rarely perceive the dangers of their jumping, kicking, twisting, lunging, starting, and stopping motions. They appreciate only short-term, slight benefits, with no notion of the consequences to come later.

Ken Hutchins is correct. Human beings have a very poor concept of time. Degenerative joint debilities will plague most aerobic exercise enthusiasts during old age. Their ability to move at all will be greatly impaired. The imposed immobility will result in poorer cardiovascular fitness than if they had totally avoided exercise during their early years.

Of course, these cripples will not admit or may not even suspect the cause and effect of their mistake. They will gleefully point to the genetic exceptions who jog and dance into their eighties without a hitch. It is likely that the next generation will simply follow suit with increased vigor justified by the same exceptions. They will never make the connection between their debilities and the fitness boom. They are just like Karo in this regard.

A decade ago Dr. Kenneth Cooper, author of *Aerobics* and *The New Aerobics*, was believed to be the man who would save everybody's heart. Now he is regarded by some as the man who destroyed everybody's knees. But is he the destroyer or are we? We did what he said. We continued to run despite the increasing incidence of injury.

A SAFE, EFFICIENT PROGRAM FOR CARDIOVASCULAR ENDURANCE

Cardiovascular fitness is extremely important. What is needed is a safe, efficient approach to developing it.

Jogging and aerobic dancing, because of the repetitive pounding and sudden movements, are not safe. Both can produce cardiovascular fitness, but not efficiently.

Swimming and cycling are safer than jogging and dancing, and they can be as productive. But neither swimming nor cycling is highly efficient, especially when compared to full-range exercise on Nautilus equipment. Full-range exercise provides quality resistance against quantity movement with maximum safety and efficiency.

Ken Hutchins supervises Karen Schmitt through a workout at a Nautilus Training Seminar. Exercising on Nautilus equipment offers a safe, efficient approach to cardiovascular fitness. (Photo by Inge Cook)

Obtaining high levels of cardiovascular endurance with Nautilus equipment requires the following planning:

1. Select any of the basic routines from Chapter 21. Approximately 12 different exercises should be used.

2. Place the appropriate selector pin in the correct weight setting on all machines before the workout begins. This facilitates your moving from one machine to the next with minimum delay.

3. Strive to perform 12 repetitions on each exercise in proper form and carry each exercise to momentary muscular failure.

4. Move quickly, preferably in less than 15 seconds, from the completion of one exercise to the beginning of the next. Your goal is to elevate your heart rate to 70–85 percent of your maximum heart rate and keep it at that level for the duration of the workout.

5. Have an instructor, training partner, or friend keep records of your repetitions and elapsed training time. Your assistant will also need to make sure you are properly pushed or paced throughout the workout. At first it is easy to become nauseated if the pace is too fast.

6. Progress in your cardiovascular training by increasing your resistance on each machine and by decreasing the time between exercises. A 12-exercise routine could take as long as 25 minutes or as little as 12 minutes, depending on your current cardiovascular condition.

7. Repeat the workout three times per week.

Nautilus training, if it is properly performed, most definitely stimulates your heart and lungs to become stronger and more enduring. It also builds high levels of muscular strength, joint flexibility, and body leanness.

11

Heredity and Training

Inherited characteristics play a dominating role in every individual's life. These inherited characteristics are transmitted from generation to generation by a complex system of genes. The study of genes is called *genetics.*

"How one thinks," Arthur Jones says, "is determined by genetics." Not only is mental capacity determined by genetics, but physical potential such as height, bodily proportions, fat, muscle mass, and other attributes come to us from our progenitors. Obviously, then, great athletes, like musicians, poets, actors, and painters, are largely born, not made.

O. J. Simpson never would have become a football superstar without the existence of somebody fleet of foot in his ancestry.

Wilt Chamberlain is certainly not the only seven-foot-tall man in the world. But his bodily proportions, neurological efficiency, skeletal formation, lack of body fat, and muscle length combined with above-average intelligence to make him the greatest basketball scorer in history.

Entirely different genes made Nadia Comaneci, at 5 feet and 87 pounds, the greatest female gymnast the world has ever seen.

All three of these famous athletes never could have attained preeminence in their special field without their inherited characteristics. But these inherited traits never would have matured without the right conditioning and coaching.

Nautilus machines are capable of furnishing correct conditioning for any athlete in any sport. But they can produce results only within the limits of the individual's inherited capabilities. Nautilus cannot make Jane Doe into a champion gymnast any more than it can make John Doe a professional basketball star.

GENETIC FACTORS

Bodily Proportions

Superior athletes have bodily proportions ideally suited to their particular sport. Dick Butkus had ideal proportions for a football middle linebacker: long torso, short legs, wide hips, narrow shoulders, and long arms. Jesse Owens had a short torso, narrow hips, long legs, and a favorable ratio of the lower to the upper leg, all of which gave him the potential to become a very fast sprinter.

Olga Korbut, former world champion gymnast, had small proportions that enabled her to perform skillfully under limited conditions. Maren Seidler, the women's national shot put champion, has large proportions that perfectly fit her sport. The bodily proportions essential to Olga would be disastrous to Maren.

From a mechanical point of view, certain bodily proportions are especially suited to each sport. Coaches and athletes need to be conscious of such inherited anatomical traits. Appropriate height, torso length, shoulder width, length of arms, leg length, and the ratio of the lower to the upper leg are crucial

Dick Butkus, shown on the Nautilus 4-way neck machine, had
the ideal combination of genetic factors for a middle
linebacker. (Photo by Inge Cook)

determinants of an individual's ability to perform.

These widths and lengths, the various attachments of tendons to bone, and the strength and musculature of the body
form its levers of locomotion. These size relationships are part
of the field of physiology called *biomechanics.*

Skeletal Formation

Skeletal formation determines bodily proportions. An athlete must possess bones large enough to support heavy
musculature. But his bones must not exceed a certain size, or
he may lose the necessary aesthetic qualities contingent upon
bone structure. The aspiring athlete with the fragile bone
structure of Woody Allen could hardly hope to develop the
heavy-duty muscles of Lou Ferrigno. Neither can an individual
with the gargantuan skeleton of Paul Anderson ever develop
the sweeping symmetry of Steve Reeves. Once a person's
bones pass a certain size, the joints tend to become so thick

that the taper of a muscle belly cannot fit into a small tight joint.

Neurological Efficiency

Neurological efficiency, as it applies to physical fitness, is the relationship between the nervous system and the muscles. The brain activates the muscles required for each movement and determines the amount of muscle power from the available supply of usable resources. People with high levels of neurological efficiency are able to contract greater percentages of their muscle masses. This places athletes with lower usable levels at a disadvantage.

Recent research undertaken in Canada reveals that neurological efficiency varies greatly among individuals. Most people were found to be able to contract, in an utmost effort, about 30 percent of a tested muscle group. A few individuals managed 40 percent; occasionally there is a 50-percent individual in neurological efficiency. Their muscles were no better or worse than those of others. They merely had the ability to contract a greater percentage of muscle fibers.

At the lower end of the normal curve is the 10-percent athlete, and for every 50-percenter, there is also a 10-percenter. Both these extremes are rare. A 50-percent individual would be a genetic freak in strength. A 10-percent person would be a "motor moron," hardly able to walk in a straight line.

These are proportional figures, but an underachieving 50-percent athlete can be beaten by a 30-percent competitor functioning neurologically at his best. The 50-percent athlete may be so accustomed to coasting that he has never learned to make a vigorous effort during training or competition. This is a major paradox limiting athletic performance. Being able to assess the potential of a player in these terms provides the coach with the knowledge of what he can expect from each member of the team. The 50-percent athlete cannot hide his potential with average performances, nor can the genetically average athlete defeat the gifted athlete with the will to work.

Muscle Length

The length of an individual's muscles is the most important factor in determining the potential size of those muscles. The longer a person's muscles, the greater the cross-sectional area and the volume of his muscles can become.

The most easily measured muscle lengths are the triceps of the arms, the gastrocnemius of the calves, and the flexors of the forearms. If two men flex the long head of the triceps, with the arm down by the side, and then measure the length of this muscle, vastly different measurements could result. The length of the first man's triceps might measure six inches, while the second man's might be nine. The length of the second man's triceps would therefore be 50 percent greater than the first man's. Consequently, the second man has the potential of 2.25 times as much cross-sectional area (1.5 × 1.5=2.25) and 3.375 as much volume or mass (1.5 × 1.5 × 1.5=3.375) to his triceps. Untrained, both these men might have approximately the same arm size, but with proper training, the second man can have much stronger and larger muscles.

The fact that a person has a short triceps does not necessarily mean that all his muscles are short. Differences are even observed between one side of the body and the other and

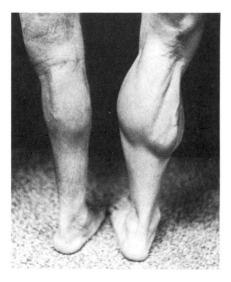

This photograph shows the difference between short and long muscles and their effect on the mass of the calf. The man on the right has greater size to his calf primarily because of his long gastrocnemius and soleus muscles. (Photo by Ellington Darden)

between body part and body part. It is the rare individual who has uniform potential over the entire body. Often we see a bodybuilder who has great arms and legs but suffers a noticeable deficiency in the torso. And there are athletes with large thighs and small calves; this is most prevalent among blacks. Most blacks inherit short gastrocnemius muscles and long tendons in their lower legs.

Body Fat

All people are born with adipose cells that specialize in accumulating fat. Many nutritional authorities think that the number of these cells is predetermined genetically. According to these authorities, family fat deposits are inherited in the same way as height, coloring, nose shapes, and muscle length.

Researchers have found that the average nonobese person has about 25–30 billion fat cells throughout his body. For the moderately obese, the number of fat cells is about 50 billion. For the extremely obese, the number of fat cells may be as high as 237 billion. Perhaps this explains why some people think they were destined to be fat or find it very difficult to lose fat permanently.

During the first year of life, cell numbers increase fairly rapidly. The total number of fat cells is about three times greater at one year of age than at birth. Scientists believe that most fat cells existing prior to birth are formed during the last three months of pregnancy. After the first year of life, cell numbers increase more gradually to the age of about 10. The number of fat cells formed continues to increase after the age of 13 and during the growth spurt of adolescence until adulthood, at which time there is little or no further increase.

Thus there appear to be three critical periods during which the number of fat cells significantly increases. The first period is during the last trimester of pregnancy, the second is during the first year of life, and the third occurs during the adolescent growth spurt.

It is during adulthood that the total number of fat cells cannot be altered. It should be pointed out, however, that there is still no substantial data to indicate clearly that the final number of adult fat cells cannot be modified through some form of intervention at an earlier period of life. If fat cells can be altered, it is likely to be accomplished by a combination of two factors: modification of early nutrition and proper exercise.

Somatotypes

Research on various body types has been done by numerous authorities. Foremost of these is Dr. W. H. Sheldon, an American scholar who categorized human beings by a system called *somatotyping*. Dr. Sheldon concluded that the infinite variety of body types could be analyzed according to three tendencies. An individual's body could be classified by analyzing to what degree each of these three variables was represented.

He named the three variables *endomorphy, mesomorphy,*

The three basic somatotypes are shown below. Left to right: endomorphy, mesomorphy, and ectomorphy. (Photo by Ellington Darden)

and *ectomorphy*. Endomorphy is the tendency to soft round-
ness in the body. Mesomorphy is the tendency to muscularity.
Ectomorphy is the tendency toward slimness.

The basic endomorph is stocky with a large round body, a
short thick neck, and short arms and legs with fatter upper
arms and thighs.

The perfect mesomorph is strongly built with broad muscular shoulders and chest, very muscular arms and legs, and little
body fat. (Other body types can develop larger muscles, but
not to the same degree as a mesomorph.)

The prototype ectomorph is tall and thin with a narrow
body, thin arms and legs, little body fat, and stringy muscles.

Dr. Sheldon drew a scale for each variable of body type. An
individual could be scored from 1 to 7 on each tendency. But
if the score was high on one, it could not be high on others. By
listing all three scores, the person's body type was recorded,
analyzed, and somatotyped.

An extreme endomorph would be 7-1-1, an extreme mesomorph 1-7-1, and an extreme ectomorph 1-1-7. In reality, such
extremes seldom occur, but neither are most people an
average 4-4-4.

Dr. Sheldon's system assumes that the somatotype does not
change with age, diet, or exercise. But some experts believe
that somatotype can be altered partially through exercise
during puberty. All agree, however, that by age 16 or 17, everybody's basic type has been permanently established.

A knowledge of which sport favors which somatotype can
guide a young athlete in choosing athletic pursuits. Somatotyping an athlete is done by analyzine three photographs using
carefully standardized postures. The scoring is a matter of
judgment, but experienced assessors rate the same body very
similarly.

INTELLIGENT TRAINING

Bodily proportions, skeletal formation, neurological efficiency, muscle length, and body fat are all genetic traits that

cannot be changed through training. Only training, however, can activate them to capacity. True, genetic qualities are limiting factors. But this is not to say that a given individual cannot improve his existing development, performance, or appearance. With strict attention to training methods, eating habits, and coaching, every person could reach the upper limits of his or her particular genetic potential.

Even the chosen few who are born with almost perfect combinations of genetic factors necessary for success in a given activity will improve faster if they approach their training intelligently. An aspiring champion, whose ultimate potential may be less than that of a mesomorphic opponent, may still achieve greater success through the use of applied intelligence. The ultimate, however, occurs when superior genetic factors are married to the intellectual capacity to utilize them. This combination cannot be beaten. Genetic factors exist and generally cannot be altered.

The following concepts summarize the importance of genetics and Nautilus training.

1. From a biomechanical point of view, certain bodily proportions and bone structures are necessary for success in building and demonstrating strength. There are also ideal bodily proportions for success in a given sport.

2. Individuals with high levels of neurological efficiency get faster results from Nautilus training. These people also have a marked advantage in competition where great muscular strength is required.

3. The mesomorphic individual has greater probability of success in Nautilus training than does the endomorphic or ectomorphic individual.

4. The length of a given muscle determines its ultimate size potential. Any athlete desiring large muscle size must be blessed with longer-than-average muscle bellies.

5. Where an individual stores fat on his body and to what degree are genetically predetermined. Many bodybuilders who are trying to obtain great muscular definition fail to realize that this may be impossible. Great muscular definition

requires not only that the individual have a low percentage of body fat but that the majority of that fat is stored on the inside of the body. Most people store the majority of their fat under the skin all over their bodies.

The superior athlete was born with the genetic possibility to be a great basketball player, tennis player, wrestler, runner, bodybuilder, or any other kind of sports performer. His training and coaching were important for his success, but not as important as his genetics.

An individual desiring to be taller might assume, after watching several professional basketball games, that bouncing a ball would make him taller. After trying various ball-bouncing routines with no success, he might conclude that bouncing a ball has no effect on his height. He might also realize that if an individual has the genetic potential to be taller, he will grow taller whether he bounces the ball or not. If he grew in height, it would be due to his genetic inheritance and not his ball bouncing.

To play professional basketball, an individual generally has to be very tall. He has to learn the skills of basketball at a young age. This is not to say, however, that all people cannot learn the skills of basketball and enjoy playing the game. But there is little probability of an individual's playing professional basketball unless he has inherited genes that make him tall.

To win the Mr. America Contest or other bodybuilding championships, an individual must first have the proper genetic potential. He must have the ideal bodily proportions and bone structure, long muscle bellies in the appropriate places, and the ability to store fat deep inside the body rather than between the skin and the muscles.

Proper Nautilus training will not make a man into a Mr. America unless he has that genetic potential, and few people do have it. But proper Nautilus training will vastly improve anyone's muscular size, strength, shape, and condition—and will do this quickly. It will not, however, make a mediocre athlete into a world champion. Champions are largely born, not made.

12

The Importance of Logic

One of the best research facilities is the human mind. Many valid answers regarding exercise can be derived with the use of sound premises and logic.

The Nautilus principles are based on accepted facts. Most of these facts are not new. They have been known to the scientific community for more than 100 years. Arthur Jones did not discover or claim to discover any of them. He merely assembled them into a logical framework to provide valid conclusions about exercise. No one had done that before.

The Nautilus philosophy is the only exercise philosophy that can be derived logically from the facts and principles of the classical sciences. Does that necessarily make Nautilus correct? No. And it does not necessarily make illogically conceived approaches to exercise wrong.

But logic does confer on Nautilus a high probability of being correct. Illogic confers on other approaches a high probability of being wrong. Why do we say "probability"?

There are two fundamental approaches to logic. One is inductive reasoning; the other is deductive reasoning.

Deductive reasoning is said to be closed-ended. It allows for no other possible answers.

Inductive reasoning is open-ended. It narrows the choices for correct conclusions, but it allows for several possible answers.

Since inductive reasoning involves choice, choosing the correct conclusion involves a certain degree of chance.

The Nautilus principles are inferred through deductive reasoning. But research into uncharted areas of exercise application are based on both preceding deductive and inductive reasoning.

Logic can be misapplied. Unknowingly, inductive reasoning is often treated deductively. Also, premises are not checked for their soundness. With unsound premises, many logical, valid, *though wrong* conclusions are derived in the exercise philosophies today. This is misuse. The logic does not fail us, however.

NAUTILUS DERIVATION

The Nautilus principles are derived from three disciplines of reference:

1. Physics
2. Biology
3. Motor Learning

Physics: The most sound premises possible are found in physics, especially mechanical physics. Concepts of physical work, velocity, momentum, force, lever, and torque are directly inferred from the field of physics and applied to Nautilus concepts.

Biology: Slightly less sound than physics, but now accepted for more than 100 years, are those concepts borrowed from biology: genetics, general physiology, muscular function, nutrition, and comparative mammalian morphology.

Motor Learning: This is a program of study found in many physical education departments. It has been an organized discipline for approximately 50 years. Motor learning deals with the processes and factors related to the acquisition and performance of movement skills. Studying a textbook on the subject by either Dr. Bryant Cratty or Dr. Robert Singer, the reader might be confused by numerous and disagreeing research models used to explain how movement skills are acquired. But deeper insight enables the reader to see that the many unique research models represent the essence of specificity. Specificity in skill practice emerges as the glaring principle shining through all motor-learning research. On the other hand, strength training and conditioning require generality.

The Nautilus principles could not have emerged without a person having a deep awareness and understanding of physics, biology, and motor learning. But still, such awareness was not enough. To build a Nautilus machine from scratch required the logical synthesis of the premises of these three disciplines.

WHY IS LOGIC UNPOPULAR?

Logic is depriving. It deprives us of choice. If it points our reasoning in the direction of unpalatable answers, we tend to deny its value:

"That can't be so."

"Let's hope for some other answer."

"This is not what I want to believe."

To reject logic is an expected reaction when discussing the Nautilus principles with the uninformed. They choose to be unreasonable. To do otherwise is to forfeit the hope of impossible results from exercise. To accept logic is to resign themselves to the fact that they really cannot exceed their genetic potential or defy laws of physics. But little do they

Much logical thinking—based on a backbone of facts from physics, biology, and motor learning—was responsible for the development of Nautilus equipment. Still, the progression from concepts and drawings to manufactured machines must go through dozens of prototypes and modifications. The picture above shows some of the experimental machines that were necessary in finally reaching production models.

realize that their cherished beliefs deny them the real benefits of exercise and invite harmful results.

Disbelief carries as much religious overtone as belief in any doctrine or philosophy. A person can be accused of possessing a Nautilus fervor just as easily as of blind faith in a mythical religion. Arthur Jones fully anticipated such reactions, pro and con, to the Nautilus principles in 1971. In a magazine article he once wrote: "Please do not *believe* in the Nautilus approach to exercise. Try to understand it."

The problem is that understanding is predicated on a certain degree of confidence. We at Nautilus Sports/Medical Industries are confident that the general approach to exercise in this book is correct. If we placed no confidence in our sources, our logical reasoning, and our ability to convey it—our approach would have no backbone. But where is that thin line where confidence becomes indistinguishable from belief? This we cannot say.

RESEARCH: CHAMPION OF TRUTH?

During the Middle Ages differences between rival parties were decided on the field of honor. Today's vogue is to decide truth by research.

Publishing studies in scientific journals lends academic credence to, or takes it away from, the theoretical propositions examined. A common attitude prevails that research proves or disproves logical conclusion. Research carries the status that it alone checks truth. When research is performed competently, this might be so.

Jim Flanagan points out to a seminar group that Nautilus equipment and concepts are based on logical reasoning.

As it often happens, research and logical reasoning disagree. This is expected when premises are unsound. But if the research is performed competently and logic is applied properly to sound premises, then no disagreement should occur.

Nautilus has participated in research in university and military as well as private settings. Research is a more haphazard affair than what most laymen suspect or scientists admit. This is especially true of research that involves human subjects.

The typical American imagines research to occur in a controlled setting with controlled substances with known values and properties. This test-tube approach does not apply well to the social sciences. And exercise research is blatantly social when it comes to human involvement.

If research is performed under the tightest control, logically, according to plans laid well in advance, and with the strictest statistical safeguards taking into account the largest known error of the measuring tools involved, then something valuable can be learned. This is most likely in the classical sciences. Only in math, chemistry, and physics do we have almost ideal—not absolute—control in research.

Once we leave this arena and go into the life sciences, some degree of control is lost. In biology, for instance, certain aspects of the cellular life process cannot be studied without somehow changing or destroying that studied process. When we leave biology to step into the social sciences of psychology and sociology, even more controls evaporate. This is why all disciplines must infer principles from the classical sciences. The classical sciences give all other disciplines their foundation.

MOVING IN THE RIGHT DIRECTION

The previous discussion of the weaknesses of research might lead you to the conclusion that all exercise-related projects should be abolished. That conclusion was not intended.

Exercise-related research must continue. But it must continue with greater attention paid to its shortcomings. Keep the

"Take what you hear," says Arthur Jones at a recent seminar, "and examine it and apply it logically to your own life."

design simple. Be curious but be skeptical. Consider specific findings with appropriate limitations, rather than broad, sweeping conclusions. Most important, don't be afraid to admit that you're wrong, that you made a mistake, and that you don't know the answer.

Arthur Jones makes an important point when he says: "Don't believe what you hear because I said it or anybody else said it. Take what you hear and examine it and apply it logically to your own life."

The exercise world could do itself and its followers a big favor by studying and applying logic. If not, exercise will never live up to its potential benefits.

The future of exercise depends on the results of trainees who can discriminate a logical approach from irrational behavior. They will literally strike it rich. Most of the others who subscribe to the more-is-better fitness mania will mine fool's gold.

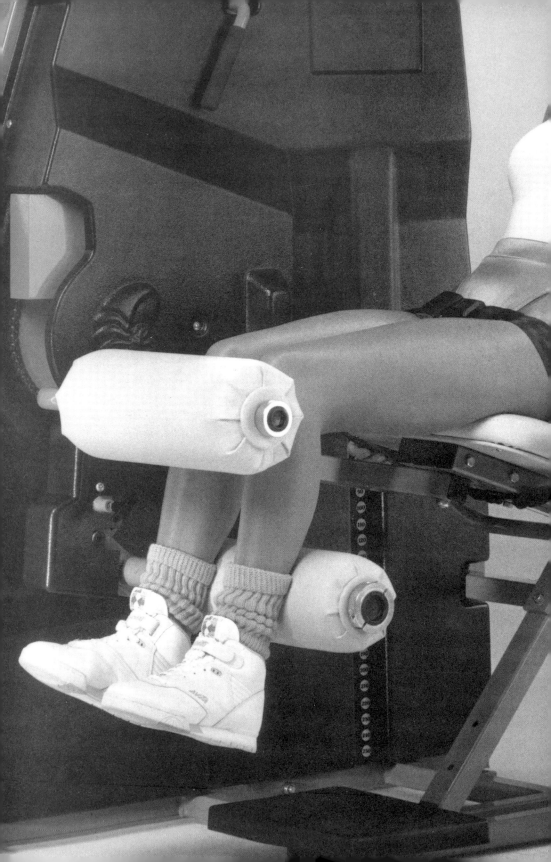

II.
Proper
Use
of Nautilus
Machines

The Next Generation seated leg curl isolates the hamstrings of the back thighs.

The Next Generation abdominal machine features a moving axis of rotation to limit the exercise to the rectus abdominis muscles.

13

The Next Generation

Before 1970 exercise machines that provided rotary, direct, variable, and balanced resistance did not exist. Nautilus Sports/Medical Industries is primarily responsible for these innovations.

Since then, dozens of exercise equipment companies have tried to copy various Nautilus machines. But none of these companies have put it all together in a way that has improved upon Arthur Jones's original concepts.

Rotary, direct, variable, and balanced resistance pioneered the strength-training boom throughout the 1970s and 1980s. These same concepts are still crucial to the Nautilus machinery that will be manufactured in the future.

The current line of commercial equipment is called Next Generation. The person most responsible for this advanced series is Greg Webb. Greg is the chief engineer in the Nautilus manufacturing plant in Independence, Virginia, where he has worked since 1980.

The Next Generation—compared to previous machines—are smoother, quieter, smaller, stronger, safer, and more efficient.

SMOOTHER AND QUIETER

The latest machines utilize anti-friction roller bearings in all rotation points. Less friction in an exercise machine means that the negative portion of the movement is heavier. Furthermore, the additional smoothness of the movement allows the performance of an extra repetition or two, which leads to more thorough muscle fiber involvement. Not only do the roller bearings reduce friction, but they also make the machines quieter and less resistant to wear.

SMALLER AND STRONGER

The Next Generation frame design incorporates the triangle within the geometric pattern. The triangle contains the highest degree of structural strength, which makes the machines smaller and lighter while increasing the frame rigidity and integrity.

MORE EFFICIENT

The variable-resistance curves for all Next Generation Nautilus machines have been reviewed and enhanced through computer technology. The cams incorporated into the new machines reinforce potential strength curves, which assures full-range development of the entire muscle structure.

Also related to efficiency is the fact that for many years all

This executive fitness center houses most of the Next Generation Nautilus machines.

lower-back and abdominal machines have rotated around a fixed axis. Only Nautilus has corrected the problem by an instantaneous center that traces the changing axis of rotation. This has been achieved through the use of a four-bar linkage system. By correctly locating the anchor points, the four-bar linkage mechanism follows the human body's rotation points during lower-back and abdominal movements.

RANGE LIMITERS

Range limiters on exercise machines allow the user to vary his starting position and thus reduce the range of movement. This can be of great advantage when rehabilitating an injury or after surgery when full-range movements are not desirable initially. Five Next Generation machines—leg extension, leg curl, pullover, abdominal, and lower back—feature the range limiters.

A major advantage of the Nautilus range limiter is the fact that when the resistance arm moves into a new position, the cam also moves to keep the resistance in proportion to the proper strength curve. Many other range limiters on the market do not rotate the cam relative to the resistance arm and thus cause the strength curve to be out of phase with the movement. Machines with out-of-phase cams can be dangerous.

SAFER

The Next Generation machines are safer because the weight stacks and most moving parts are shielded. The shields are made of durable plastic, which helps to reduce maintenance.

HOW-TO APPLICATIONS

Over 20 different Next Generation machines are pictured and described, as are many of the older versions, in the following nine chapters. With proper application of the directions given, you should be able to improve significantly the shape and condition of your body.

The duo hip and back machine provides full-range exercise for the largest, strongest muscle of the body: the gluteus maximus.

14
Hips

In Nautilus fitness centers across the country, people are mistakenly confusing the reduction of the hips with developing a big bottom. The hips and buttocks are among the most misunderstood parts of the human body.

Should the size of these muscles be reduced or increased?

Should women exercise the buttocks in a fashion different from men?

Is sitting the primary purpose of the buttocks?

The answer to these questions comes from an understanding of human anatomy.

FUNCTION OF THE BUTTOCKS

The buttocks are used for sitting, since their covering is a thick layer of fatty tissue that acts as a natural cushion. The primary function of the buttocks, however, is not sitting, but the forceful extension of the hip. This forceful extension of the hip is controlled by the largest and strongest muscles of the body, the gluteus maximus. All running, jumping, squatting, and intensive pushing is made possible by the gluteus maximus muscles.

All those involved in running and jumping sports can improve their performance by strengthening the gluteal muscles. Women concerned about the appearance of the buttocks area can, by keeping the gluteus maximus muscles as strong as possible, create a dimple-free sleekness to the overlying skin. Those who are troubled by lower back pain can add considerable support to the back and spinal column by keeping the buttocks in strong condition.

If, by chance, someone developed the muscles of the buttocks to a disproportionate degree, then lack of activity for several days would result in automatic atrophy of the unused muscles. Muscles that are increased in size and strength through exercise do not remain in that condition unless they are frequently taxed to their limits.

Women who are concerned with overly fat hips should understand that this has little to do with large gluteus maximus muscles. This state is usually the result of an inherited tendency in many women to store above-average amounts of fat on the backsides of their bodies. If this is the case, and it will be with numerous women, the proper combination of diet and exercise can correct the condition. But it will not alter anyone's tendency to be disproportionately fat in the hips.

Women should train in the same way as men, using the same exercises, repetitions, and sets. A woman's muscles should be treated exactly the same as a man's.

NAUTILUS HIP AND BACK MACHINE

The Nautilus hip and back machine was one of the first pieces of exercise equipment that Arthur Jones designed. The early model consisted of a single movement arm, the resistance had to be supplied by barbell plates, and there was no get-in/get-out device. It took several strong people to pull the movement arm to the contracted position as the trainee positioned himself on the axes of rotation and buckled down.

Since 1970 there have been at least a dozen improvements of the original hip and back machine. The current model, called duo hip and back, is much safer than some of the earlier versions, and it offers even better results.

OTHER NAUTILUS HIP MACHINES

Two machines have recently been designed for the hip area. The Nautilus hip abduction machine provides full-range exercise for the gluteus medius muscles of the outer hips, and the Nautilus hip flexion machine works the iliopsoas muscles of the front hip area. These machines, when used in conjunction with the hip and back machine, effectively strengthen and shape a neglected part of the female and male anatomies.

Duo Hip and Back

1. Enter machine from the front by separating movement arms.

2. Lie on your back with both legs over roller pads.

3. Align hip joint with axes of cams.

4. Fasten seat belt and grasp handles lightly. Seat belt should be snug but not too tight, as back must be arched at completion of movement.

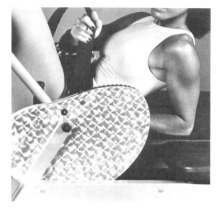

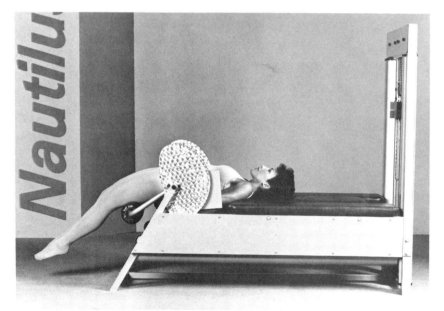

5. Extend both legs and at the same time push back with arms. With a heavy weight, extend one leg and hold it in the down position. Extend the other leg to the same position.

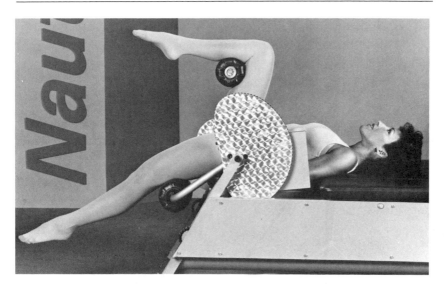

6. Keep one leg at full extension. Allow other leg to bend and come back as far as possible.

7. Stretch.

8. Push out until it joins the other leg at extension.

9. Pause, arch lower back, and contract buttocks. In contracted position, keep legs straight, knees together, and toes pointed.

10. Repeat with the other leg and continue alternating one leg with the other.

Hip Abduction
(Next Generation)

1. Sit in machine and place legs on movement arms. (Some small individuals may require an extra back pad and additional thigh pads.)
2. Fasten seat belt.
3. Keep head and shoulders against seat back.

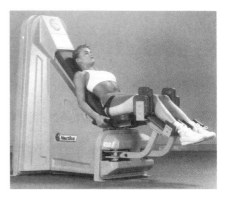

4. Push knees and thighs laterally to widest position.
5. Pause.
6. Return to knees-together position.
7. Repeat.

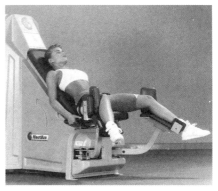

Hip Flexion

1. Sit in machine.
2. Fasten belt across thighs.
3. Lie back in reclining position.
4. Grasp handles.
5. Keep torso and head on seat back.
6. Flex hips smoothly by drawing knees to chest.
7. Pause.
8. Lower slowly to starting position.
9. Repeat.

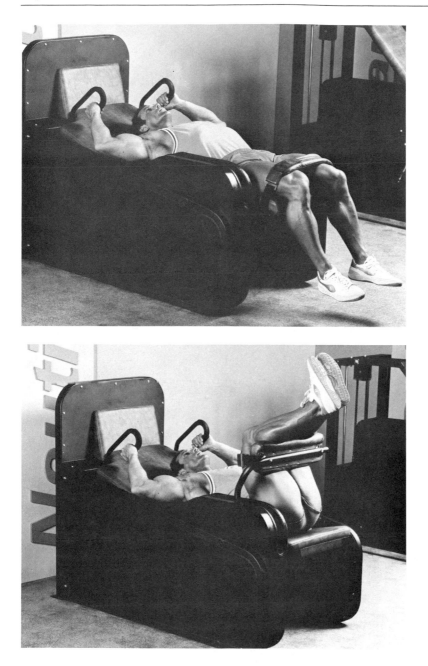

The frontal thighs or quadriceps are brought into action on the Next Generation leg extension.

15

Legs

The leg is a marvelous structure. Long, lean, and shapely, a symmetrical pair of legs can go a long way toward bringing their owner fame on the athletic field, recognition on the dance floor, or admiration on the beach.

The leg, unfortunately, is one of the most vulnerable parts of the body. Almost everyone has suffered from ankle sprains. While ankle sprains are seldom permanently disabling, a knee injury can end an athlete's career as fast as he can say, "crackback block."

The knee is the largest and most complex joint of the body. A multiplicity of ligaments gives the knee its stability. Crossing on top of the ligaments are the important muscles and tendons of the thigh and calf. There is no way to strengthen ligaments and tendons without working the muscles that connect and surround them.

The muscles of the legs must be kept strong to protect the

joints from injury. Strong legs not only prevent injuries but also improve performance in any running and jumping activity. Strong legs also contribute to overall fitness and body appearance.

KNEE AND THIGH

Although the knee is the largest joint in the body, from an architectural point of view it is one of the weakest. Its structural weakness is due to the fact that in no position of flexion or extension are the bones ever in more than partial contact. This is especially important to the athlete because the knees support his weight, and stopping and starting movements put tremendous pressure on the knee joints.

The knee is essentially a hinge held together by a system of ligaments and tendons. There are 13 distinct ligaments that enter into its strength and support.

Of equal importance are a number of powerful muscles that cross the knee. The four muscles of the quadriceps and the three muscles of the hamstrings provide a tripod effect around the knee joint. Strong quadriceps and hamstrings muscles offer the first line of defense against injury. The large muscles of the quadriceps and hamstrings also contribute to the size and strength of the thigh.

Five muscles compose the medial or inner thigh. Of these muscles, the adductor magnus is the largest. The adductor magnus has its origin on the pubis bone and inserts along the entire length of the thigh bone. Contraction of the adductor magnus and other inner thigh muscles brings the thighs from a spread-legged to a knees-together position. This movement is called *hip adduction*.

ANKLE AND CALF

In some ways the ankle joint functionally resembles the knee. Both joints bear most of the body's weight, allow motion predominately in the same direction, are supported by strong ligaments on either side, and are occasionally injured and later reinjured.

Bones and ligaments are the ankles' chief stability. Every aspect of the ankle is supported by a maze of ligaments and is arranged to offer maximum support with maximum mobility. The strongest sets of ligaments are on the medial (inside) and lateral (outside) sides of the ankle. The ligaments restrict excess foot inversion and eversion. When the ligaments are damaged, so is the ability to maintain proper ankle stability, and recurrent sprains are a result.

Muscle tendons that cross the ankle on either side also aid in stabilization. On the medial side, the posterior tibial tendon offers ankle support, while on the lateral side the peroneal tendons exert their force.

The rounded form of the calf is primarily a result of the mass of two muscles, the gastrocnemius and the soleus. These muscles insert into the heel bone by way of the Achilles tendon. They also cross the back of the knee joint. The gastroc-soleus muscles are the prime mover for ankle extension, and they assist the hamstrings in knee flexion.

Leg Extension

1. Sit in machine.
2. Place feet behind roller pads.
3. Adjust seat back to comfortable position.
4. Fasten seat belt across hips.
5. Keep head and shoulders against seat back.
6. Grasp handles lightly.
7. Straighten both legs smoothly.
8. Pause.
9. Lower resistance slowly.
10. Repeat

Leg Extension (Next Generation)

1. Sit in machine.
2. Lean forward and place shins behind roller pad.
3. Adjust seat back to buttocks.
4. Make sure knees are aligned with axis of rotation of movement arm. Axis is marked with a red dot.
5. Fasten seat belt.

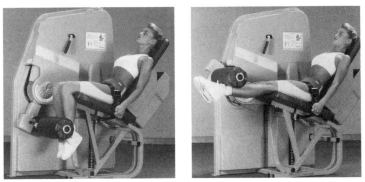

6. Push movement arm forward and upward. Be sure to reach full knee extension. Grasp handles for stability during last half of extension.
7. Pause at full extension.
8. Lower movement arm until weight stack barely touches.
9. Repeat.

Range Limiter
- Push release handle and hold.
- Shuttle movement arm to new starting position; stop, then release handle.
- Do not push release handles if weights are raised.
- Reset machine by pushing release handle after lowering weights. Allow movement arm to return to zero degree starting position. Release handle.

Adjustable Movement Arm
- Pull release handle on movement arm.
- Move leg pad to desired position: low, normal, or high. Release handle and make sure pin locks securely.

Duo Squat

1. Sit on lower portion of seat. Shoulders should be under pads.

2. At the same time, place both feet on movement arms. Heels should be on bottom of foot pedals.

3. Pull up on lower right handle to adjust seat carriage. Seat is in proper position when these three factors occur as both legs straighten: (a) cam fully unwinds; (b) movement arms touch crossbar; and (c) legs can barely lock out.

4. Straighten both legs.

5. Hold left leg straight while right leg bends slowly and comes back as far as possible.

6. Push out smoothly with right leg until straight.

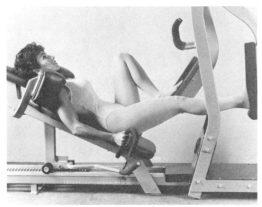

7. Hold right leg straight and bend left leg.

8. Push out smoothly with left leg until straight.

9. Alternate between right and left legs until fatigued.

Duo Leg Press

1. Sit on seat bottom.
2. Place both feet on movement arms. Heels should be on bottom of foot pedals.
3. Pull up on lower right handle to adjust seat carriage. Seat is in proper position when these three factors occur as both legs straighten: (a) cams fully unwind; (b) movement arms touch crossbar; and (c) legs can barely lock out.

4. Straighten both legs.
5. Hold left leg straight while right leg bends slowly and comes back as far as possible.
6. Push out smoothly with right leg until straight.
7. Hold right leg straight and bend left leg.
8. Push out smoothly with left leg until straight.
9. Alternate between right and left legs until fatigued.

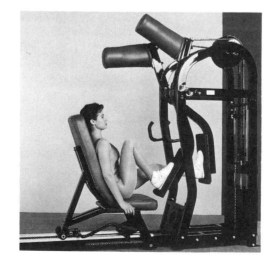

Leg Curl

1. Lie facedown on machine.
2. Place feet under roller pads with knees just over edge of bench. (Some people may require an extra pad under their thighs to put knees in proper alignment with axis.)
3. Grasp handles to keep body from moving.

4. Curl legs and try to touch heels to buttocks.
5. Lift hips to increase range of movement.
6. Pause at point of full muscular contraction.
7. Lower resistance slowly.
8. Repeat.

Seated Leg Curl (Next Generation)

1. Sit in machine.
2. Place legs between two roller pads. The end pad should be behind ankles and the other pad in front of shins, just below knees.
3. Align knee joints with axis of rotation of movement arm. Axis is marked with a red dot.
4. Pull seat back forward to buttocks.
5. Fasten seat belt across hips and grasp handles lightly.

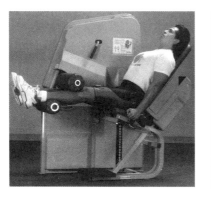 

6. Curl legs and try to touch heels to buttocks.
7. Lower movement arm until weight stack barely touches.
8. Repeat.

Range Limiter
- Push release handle and hold.
- Shuttle movement arm to new starting position; stop, then release handle.
- Do not push release handle if weights are raised.
- Reset machine by pushing release handle after lowering weights. Allow movement arm to return to zero degree starting position. Release handle.

Adjustable Movement Arm
- Pull release handle on movement arm.
- Move leg pad to desired position: low, normal, or high. Release handle and make sure pin locks securely.

Hip Adduction (Next Generation)

1. Adjust lever on right side of machine for range of movement.

2. Sit in machine and place knees and ankles on movement arm in a spread-legged position. The inner thighs and knees should be firmly against resistance pads. (Some small individuals may need an extra back pad.)

3. Fasten seat belt.

4. Keep head and shoulders against back seat.

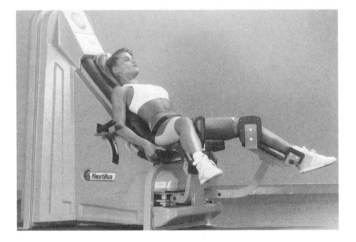

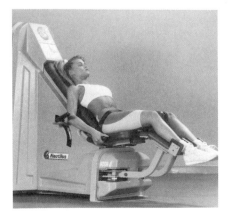

5. Pull knees and thighs together smoothly. To isolate adductor muscles better, keep feet pointed inward and pull with thighs, not lower legs.

6. Pause in knees-together position.

7. Return to stretched position slowly.

8. Repeat.

Calf Raise on Multi-Exercise

1. Adjust belt on multi-exercise machine comfortably around hips.

2. Place balls of feet on first step and hands on front of carriage.

3. Lock knees and keep locked throughout movement.

4. Elevate heels as high as possible and try to stand on big toes.

5. Pause.

6. Lower heels slowly.

7. Stretch at bottom by lifting and spreading toes.

8. Repeat.

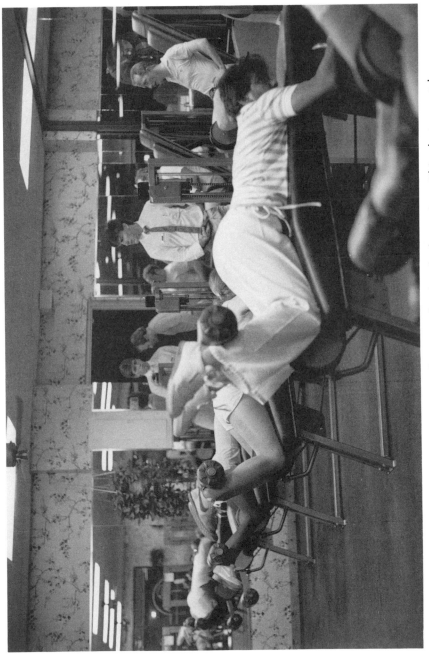

The Nautilus leg curl is one of the best exercises for strengthening the hamstrings. This photo was taken at the Gainesville Health and Fitness Center in Gainesville, Florida. (Photo by Ken Hutchins)

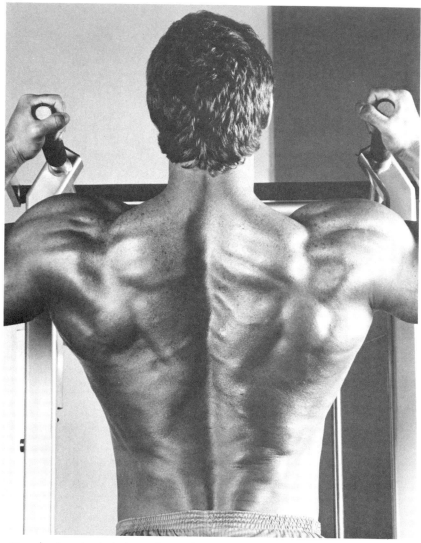

Developing the latissimus dorsi, the largest muscle of the upper body, contributes a dramatic V-shape to the back.

16
Back

Strength-training experts have generally agreed that the full squat, more than any other barbell exercise, produces overall gains in size and strength. These results are not limited to the legs; overall gains are noticeable in the chest, back, and arms.

Since the squat is primarily a lower-body exercise, it is no surprise that the greatest results are made in the legs. The upper body, however, does not respond to any type of barbell training as fast as the legs do to squats.

In the April 1970 issue of *Iron Man* magazine, Arthur Jones published an article entitled, "The Upper-Body Squat." In this early Jones article the athletic world was offered an exercise that would eventually revolutionize upper-body training. "The upper-body squat now exists," Jones wrote, "and it will do for the upper body just what squats have long done for the thighs."

MUSCLES OF THE BACK

Jones's upper-body squat was the first successful method of providing direct exercise for the largest, strongest muscles of the upper body, the latissimus dorsi. These muscles join to the lower part of the spine and sweep up to the armpit, where they are inserted into the upper arm bone. When the latissimus dorsi muscles contract they pull the upper arms from an overhead position down and around the shoulder axes. This rotational movement can take place with the upper arms in front of the body or at the sides of the body.

Several smaller back muscles also assist the latissimus dorsi in moving the upper arms. The most important of these muscles is the teres major.

Effectively placing the resistance on the elbows, as opposed to the hands as in conventional exercises, Jones's machine exposed the lats to direct resistance for the first time. "In six weeks," Jones wrote, "we built one subject's lats to a point that would have normally required at least two full years of training."

The original upper-body squat was performed on a machine that would be considered crude today. Despite that consideration, Peary Rader, editor of the magazine, has said that Jones's "upper-body squat" article generated more mail than any other in the history of the publication. Jones included no photographs with his manuscript. It is open speculation whether that detracted from or actually stimulated interest in his new machine.

Today the Nautilus latissimus machines consist of the pullover (several versions), behind neck, and behind neck pulldown.

Pullover (Next Generation)

1. Adjust seat so shoulders are aligned with axes of rotation of movement arm. Axes are marked with red dots.

2. Fasten seat belt and press foot pedal to move elbow pads forward.

3. Place arms on elbow pads and put hands against curved portion of crossbar. Keep hands open.

4. Remove feet from pedal and rotate elbows up and back.

5. Stretch moderately by allowing elbows to go as far back as is comfortable.

6. Rotate elbows forward until bar touches midsection.

7. Pause. Keep neck muscles relaxed. Look straight ahead or slightly downward, but keep head basically motionless.

8. Return slowly to stretched position.

9. Repeat.

10. Exit machine by pressing foot pedal to support resistance.

Women's Pullover

1. Adjust seat so shoulder joints are in line with axes of cams.

2. Assume erect position and fasten seat belt tightly.

3. Leg-press foot pedal until elbow pads are at about chin level.

4. Place elbows on pads. Hands should be open and resting on curved portion of bar.

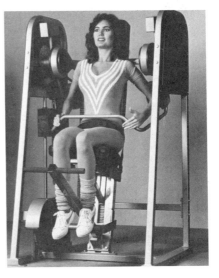

5. Remove legs from pedal and slowly rotate elbows as far back as possible.

6. Stretch.

7. Rotate elbows downward until bar touches midsection.

8. Pause.

9. Return slowly to stretched position.

10. Repeat.

Behind Neck

1. Adjust seat so shoulder joints are in line with axes of cams.
2. Fasten seat belt.
3. Place backs of upper arms, triceps area, between padded movement arms.
4. Cross forearms behind neck.

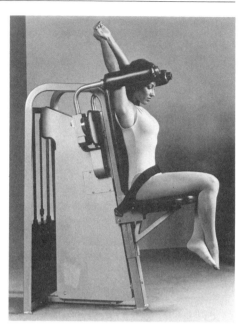

5. Move both arms downward until roller pads touch torso. Be careful not to bring arms or hands to front of body.
6. Pause.
7. Return slowly to crossed-arm position behind neck.
8. Repeat.

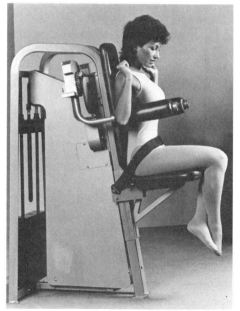

Behind Neck Pulldown on Torso Arm

1. Adjust seat so hands are barely able to grasp overhead bar.
2. Fasten seat belt.
3. Lean forward and grasp overhead bar with parallel grip.
4. Pull bar behind neck, keeping elbows back.
5. Pause.
6. Return slowly to starting position.
7. Repeat.

Pulldown on Torso Arm (Next Generation)

1. Adjust seat so hands are barely able to grasp overhead handles.
2. Fasten seat belt.
3. Grasp overhead handles with parallel grip.

4. Pull handles to shoulders.
5. Pause.
6. Return slowly to stretched position.
7. Repeat.

Compound Rowing (Next Generation)

1. Straddle seat and, while standing, lean forward and grasp the upper handles with a parallel grip.

2. Sit on seat and allow arms to stretch forward. Arms should be on a slight decline. If not, adjust seat.

3. Pull handles to sides of chest. Do not lean back. Keep upper body stationary.

4. Pause.

5. Lower resistance slowly to stretched position.

6. Repeat.

Strong, well-developed shoulders are important for success in many sports.

17
Shoulders

Shoulders are essential to success in athletics. Throwing a ball and swinging a bat, a tennis racquet, or a golf club are not feats for weak shoulders. The shoulder muscles are essential in swimming. In gymnastics and wrestling the strength of the shoulders is often the determining factor in success. Even in sprinting the limiting factor may not be leg speed but arm speed, for the shoulder muscles play an important role in moving the arms.

Being traditionally weak in the upper body, most women have more to gain from proper shoulder strengthening exercises than do men. Bony shoulders not only look unattractive but also can be the weak link in any activity that involves the arms.

The shoulders are the key to many whole-body movements. They allow for smooth coordination between the torso and the arms. They are instrumental in transferring the whole bodily power to a specific object such as a racquet. The shoulder muscles are the element transferring body power into the arms, which along with hip rotation make a powerful swing. Stronger shoulders mean that an athlete can hit a ball hard and with expert efficiency.

Once you understand the essential role of the shoulders, you can see why it is important that they be kept strong at all times. Exceptional development of the shoulder muscles will give an individual an advantage over his or her opponents, no matter what the activity. It will also add extra protection against various types of upper body injuries.

ANATOMY AND FUNCTION OF THE SHOULDERS

Movements of the shoulder joint are produced by 11 muscles. The most important of these muscles in size and shape is the deltoid. The deltoid, a triangular muscle, is on the shoulder with one angle pointing down the arm and the other two bent around the shoulder to the front and rear.

The deltoid muscle is a single mass, but it is divided into three sections: anterior, middle, and posterior. Each is involved in moving the upper arm. The anterior deltoids lift the arms forward. The middle deltoids move them sideways. The posterior deltoids lift them backward.

Because of the separate functions of the deltoids, specific exercises should be used to develop all three sections. This assures symmetrical development and protects the shoulder joint from injury.

Lateral Raise
(Next Generation)

1. Adjust seat so shoulder joints are in line with axes of cams. Axes are marked with red dots.

2. Fasten seat belt.

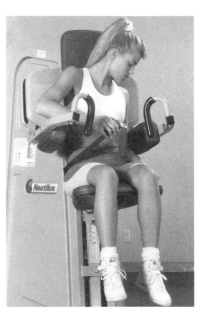

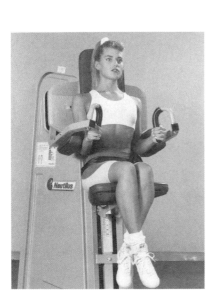

3. Grasp handles and pull back.

4. Make sure upper arms are slightly behind torso and firmly against pads.

5. Raise elbows smoothly to about chin level.

6. Pause.

7. Lower slowly to sides.

8. Repeat.

Overhead Press (Next Generation)

1. Raise seat for greatest range of movement.
2. Fasten seat belt.
3. Grasp handles above shoulders.
4. Press handles overhead while being careful not to arch lower back.
5. Lower resistance slowly, keeping elbows wide.
6. Repeat.

Double Shoulder, Lateral Raise

1. Adjust seat so shoulder joints are in line with axes of cams.
2. Position thighs on seat, cross ankles, and fasten seat belt.
3. Grasp handles lightly.

4. Lead with elbows and raise both arms to about ear level. Keep knuckles against pads and elbows high at all times.
5. Pause.
6. Lower resistance slowly and repeat. After final repetition, immediately do overhead press.

**Double Shoulder,
Overhead Press**

1. Quickly raise seat
for greater range of
movement.
2. Grasp handles
above shoulders.

3. Press handles overhead
while being careful not to
arch back.
4. Lower resistance slowly,
keeping elbows wide.
5. Repeat.

Rowing Torso

1. Sit with back toward weight stack. Some individuals may need an extra pad in front.

2. Place arms between roller pads and cross arms.

3. Bend arms in rowing fashion as far back as possible. Keep arms parallel to floor.

4. Pause.

5. Return slowly to starting position.

6. Repeat.

70° Shoulder

1. Sit in machine. Adjust seat bottom so top of shoulders are in line with axes of cams.

2. Fasten seat belt.

3. Place upper arms under roller pads. Pads should be in crook of elbows or on the lower portion of biceps.

4. Extend head and rest it on pad behind shoulders. You should be looking at ceiling.

5. Move both arms in rotary fashion until roller pads almost touch over face.
6. Pause.
7. Lower slowly to starting position.
8. Repeat.

Reverse Pullover (Next Generation)

1. Adjust seat so shoulders are aligned with axes of rotation of movement arm. Axes are marked with red dots.
2. Fasten seat belt.
3. Position hands behind handles of movement arm.
4. Rotate arms forward and upward.
5. Pause.
6. Return to starting position.
7. Repeat.

The women's chest machine supplies progressive exercise for the pectoral muscle.

18

Chest

Men and women alike have long admired a firm, shapely chest. This may account for the fact that most Americans are dissatisfied with their chest development.

Every American woman is aware that she lives in a culture that places an extraordinary emphasis on female breasts. Men interested in exercise usually have at least two goals in mind: big arms and a big chest. Regardless of sex, these individuals feel their chest is too small, too large, too flabby, too flat, or too weak—but seldom just right.

Until the Nautilus double chest machine was designed and built in 1973 no exercise worked the chest muscles without involving the weaker muscles of the upper arms. Conventional exercises for the chest, such as barbell bench presses and dumbbell flies, are dependent on the strength of the triceps. Since the triceps are much smaller and weaker than the pectoralis major muscles of the chest, the triceps fatigued long before the pectorals could be worked fully.

By placing the resistance on the elbows rather than on the hands, the Nautilus double chest machine bypassed the weaker muscles of the arms. The pectoral muscles could be worked directly. Direct resistance for these muscles would now allow people to make significant progress in attaining a strong, shapely chest.

MUSCLES OF THE CHEST

Although there are numerous muscles surrounding the chest area, the pectoralis major is the most important. It is the large fan-shaped muscle lying across the front of the chest. One end of this muscle is attached to the sternum and the other to the front of the upper arm. When the pectoral muscles contract they move the upper arms across the body. Up to this point, the male and female physical makeup is relatively the same. However, while a woman's breasts are attached to the pectoralis major muscles, they are not composed of muscle tissue. Breasts are composed of fatty tissue, milk glands, connective tissue, and blood vessels. The only muscles in the female breast are in the erectile portion of the nipple, and they have no potential for development.

Little can be done to increase the size of the female breast, outside of hormone treatments, silicone injections, surgery, or a large increase or decrease in body fat. Proper exercise, however, can definitely expand and increase the strength and tone of the underlying and surrounding muscle structures. As a result, the breasts will become firmer so they protrude more or are carried higher on the chest. Loose skin will also become tauter from proper exercise, and posture will be improved. A woman's bustline will take on new shape and contours as a result of improved tone and strength in the chest muscles.

Men can improve the tone of the muscles of the chest and develop its muscular size and strength. This is mainly because certain hormones are present in greater quantities in the male than in the female.

Double Chest, Arm Cross (Next Generation)

1. Adjust seat to align shoulders directly above axes of movement arms. Axes are marked with red dots.
2. Fasten seat belt.
3. Place forearms behind and firmly against movement arm pads.
4. Grasp handles lightly with thumbs around handles.
5. Keep head against seat back.

6. Push with forearms and try to touch elbows together in front of chest.
7. Pause.
8. Lower resistance slowly and repeat. After final repetition, immediately do decline press.

Double Chest, Decline Press (Next Generation)

1. Stay seated in machine with seat at same height.
2. Use foot pedal to raise handles into starting position.
3. Keep head back and torso erect.
4. Grasp handles with parallel grip.

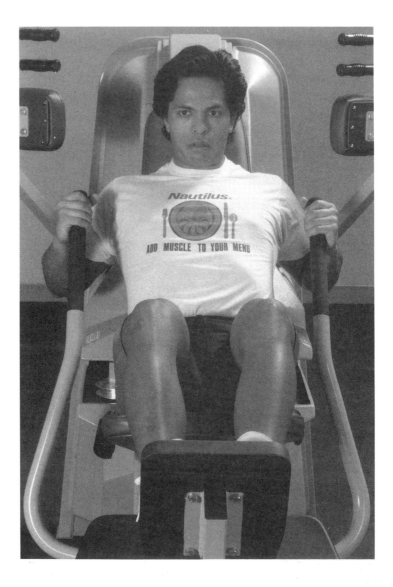

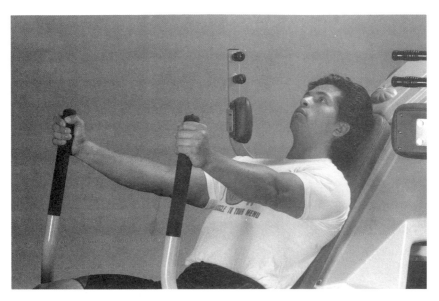

5. Press handles forward in controlled fashion.
6. Lower resistance slowly, keeping elbows wide.
7. Stretch in bottom position, then continue pressing movement.
8. Repeat.

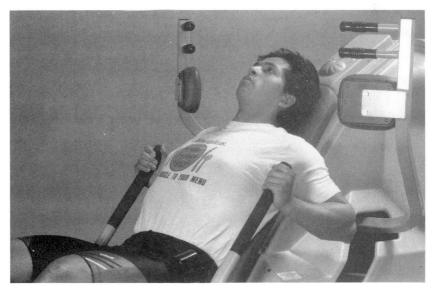

Women's Chest and Men's Chest (Next Generation)

The axes of rotation of the cams are farther apart on the men's machine than on the women's. Both machines are used in the same manner.

1. Adjust seat to align shoulders directly above axes of movement arms. Axes are marked with red dots.
2. Fasten seat belt.
3. Place forearms behind and firmly against movement arm pads.
4. Grasp handles lightly with thumbs around handles.
5. Keep head against seat back.

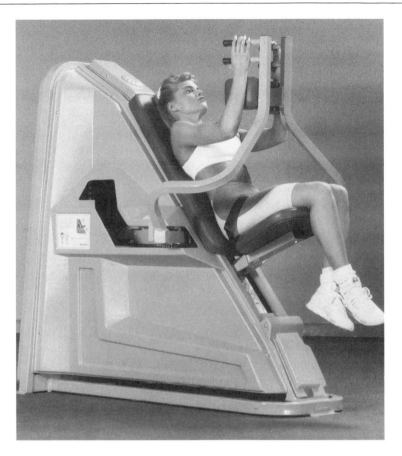

6. Push with forearms and try to touch elbows together in front of chest.

7. Pause.

8. Lower resistance slowly.

9. Repeat.

Duo Decline Press (Next Generation)

1. Sit in machine. Place feet on foot pad and push to bring handles forward.

2. Grasp handles lightly just beneath shoulders, applying pressure with palms. If handles are too high or too low, adjust seat bottom.

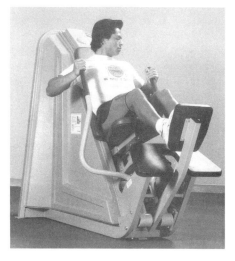

3. Remove feet from foot pad, allowing resistance to be placed on machine's movement arms.

4. Press both movement arms simultaneously. As arms straighten, keep neck back, chin down, chest up, shoulders down, and elbows slightly out.

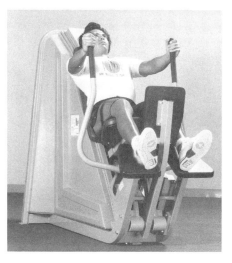

5. Lower resistance,
keeping hands even.
   6. Repeat.
   7. Exit machine by
pushing foot pad to remove
resistance from movement
arms.

8. Movement can also be
performed one arm at a
time or in an alternating
fashion.

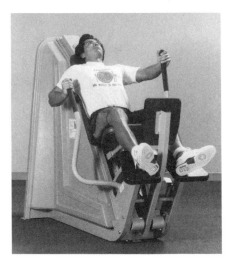

Bench Press (Next Generation)

1. Lie face up on bench with handles beside chest.
2. Grasp handles lightly. Stabilize body by placing feet flat on floor or on step provided.

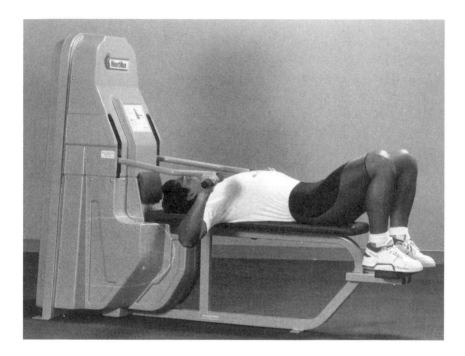

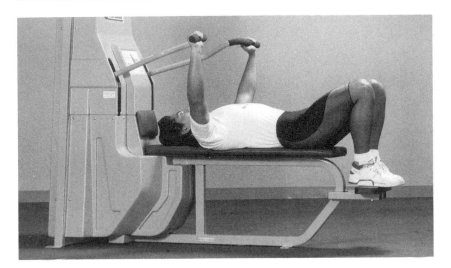

3. Press handles upward smoothly.
4. Do not jam into forceful lockout.

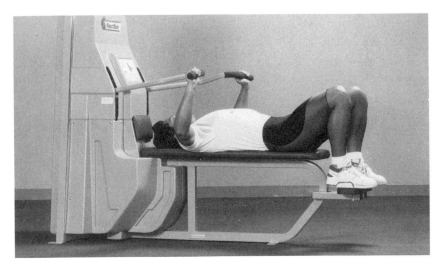

5. Lower slowly to bottom.
6. Repeat.

10° Chest

1. Lie on back with head higher than hips. Adjust torso until shoulders are in line with axes of cams.

2. Place upper arms under roller pads. Pads should be in crook of elbows.

3. Move both arms in rotary fashion until roller pads touch over chest.

4. Pause.

5. Lower slowly to starting position.

6. Repeat.

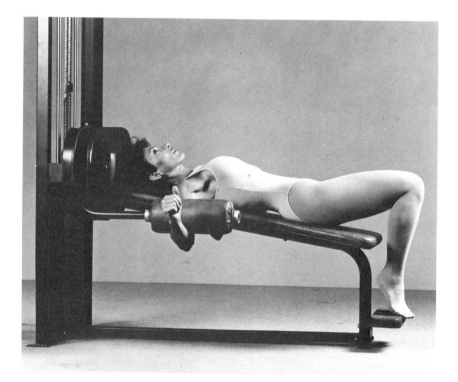

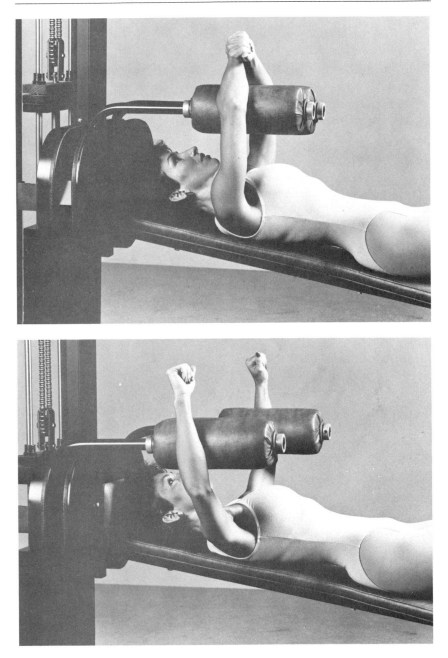

50° Chest/Shoulder (Next Generation)

1. Sit in machine. Adjust seat so tops of shoulders are aligned with axes of cams. Axes are marked with red dots.
2. Fasten seat belt.
3. Place upper arms under roller pads. Pads should be in crooks of elbows.

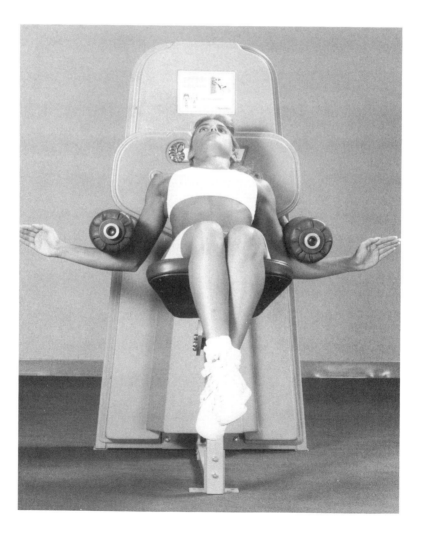

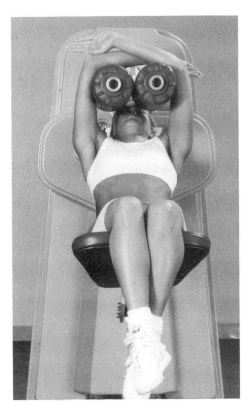

4. Move pads over face until they touch.

5. Pause.

6. Lower slowly to starting position.

7. Repeat.

Strong arms are important for fitness-minded women and men.

19
Arms

In 1973 Arthur Jones still believed that the previous generation of bodybuilders, those of the 1940s and 1950s, were rational men. After a number of such men had appeared at the Nautilus headquarters, however, Jones was beginning to wonder. One Mr. America candidate of the 1940s whose massive arms were a special status symbol in his heyday arrived. Even the great Sergio Oliva, whose arms were as big as his own head, exclaimed, "They're too big!" when shown a picture of the man's arms.

A young athlete on the Nautilus staff, anxious to learn his scientific techniques, asked the man simply, "What is the secret to building big arms?"

Without hesitation the soft-spoken man with the enormous arms answered, "You know, young man, that the muscles are comprised mostly of water. Therefore you must train your arms with the heaviest weight possible, then you must drink at least a gallon of water during and just after your workout, and finally you must pray that God will direct the water to your arms."

Arthur Jones is now convinced that bodybuilders of the 1940s and 1950s incorporated as much myth and superstition in their training as current bodybuilders do.

OLD MYTHS STILL LINGER

One prominent myth is the belief that with the so-called bombing and blitzing methods made popular by bodybuilding magazines, anyone can develop championship arms. Less than 1 percent of the male population in this country have the genetic potential to develop the arm size of a Mr. America winner. Anyone can build larger and stronger arms, but unless he has long muscle bellies in his biceps and triceps, really large muscular upper arms are an impossibility.

Even though many coaches and athletes are aware of the benefits of strength training for the arms, some still cling to the old myth that resistance exercise slows coordination and speed of limbs. They still think that "muscle-bound" is an actual condition. Strength training will not make an individual slow and clumsy or muscle-bound. This has been proven by scientific research.

Another myth is the misunderstanding that muscles are made almost wholly of protein and to build large muscles a person must consume massive amounts of protein foods. (That 1940s Mr. America competitor was at least correct when he stated that most of a muscle is water. Seventy percent of a muscle is water and only 22 percent protein.) Even before a muscle is to be nourished, there must be growth stimulation at the basic cellular level. After puberty, growth stimulation occurs in almost direct porportion to the intensity of the exercise. High-intensity exercise results in maximum degrees of growth stimulation. This growth will occur if the stimulated muscle is allowed at least 48 hours of rest. Nutrition is definitely secondary to the high-intensity exercise and rest requirements. All the body requires is a few nutrients which it can easily obtain from fat stores, and water.

MUSCLES OF THE ARMS

The biceps is the prominent muscle on the front side of the upper arm. It is a two-headed muscle made up of a long and a short head. The tendons at the top end cross the shoulder joint and are attached to the scapula. At the other end the tendons cross the elbow and are connected to the forearm just below the joint. The biceps cross two joints, the shoulder and the elbow.

The functions of the biceps are threefold. It supinates the hand, flexes the elbow, and lifts the upper arm forward. For the biceps to contract fully, the hand must be supinated, the elbow must be bent, and the upper arm must be raised to ear level.

The triceps is on the back side of the upper arm and, as its name implies, has three separate heads: lateral, medial, and long. Like the biceps, the triceps tendons cross both the shoulder and the elbow joint.

The major function of the triceps is to straighten the elbow. It also assists in bringing the upper arm down from an overhead position. For the triceps to be contracted fully, the upper arm must be behind the torso as the elbow straightens.

Nineteen separate muscles make up the forearm. These muscles act on both the fingers and the wrist. The bulk of the musculature is concentrated in two masses just below the elbow joint. The mass on the outside is formed by the bellies of the extensor muscles. The inside mass of the forearm comes from the bellies of the flexor muscles.

The forearms are a very complex structure. Disregarding the

flexion of the forearm against the upper arm, which is caused primarily by the biceps of the upper arm, the functions of the forearm are as follows: supination of the hand, pronation of the hand, gripping, extending the fingers, and bending the hand in four separate directions.

Biceps Curl (Plateloading)

1. Enter machine from left side.
2. Place elbows on pad and in line with axes of cam.
3. Grasp bar with hands together and palms up. Lean back at full extension to assure stretching.

4. Smoothly curl bar until it reaches neck.
5. Pause.
6. Return slowly to stretched position.
7. Repeat.

Multi-Biceps Curl (Next Generation)

1. Sit on seat and place elbows on padded support, but do not yet grasp handles. The seat should be at a height that places elbows slightly lower than shoulders. Stand to adjust accordingly.

2. Lean over elbow support from a standing position and grasp handles. Pull handles upward and place elbows on axes of rotation. Axes are marked with red dots.

3. Be seated.

4. Place feet flat on floor and keep legs relaxed throughout exercise.

5. Cup hands around handles instead of grasping them tightly.

6. Lower resistance until arms are straight. Do not hunch shoulders.

7. Curl both arms simultaneously as far as possible.

8. Pause.

9. Lower resistance slowly with both arms.

10. Repeat.

11. Exit machine by standing and lowering handles.

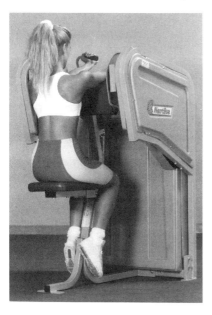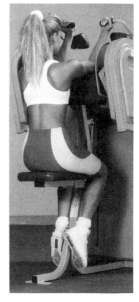

Compound Position Biceps

1. Adjust seat so elbow is in line with axis of cam. Machine has two identical seats as each arm is worked separately.
2. Sit in machine.
3. Grasp overhead handle.

4. Curl handle to shoulder.
5. Pause.
6. Lower slowly.
7. Repeat.
8. Change side and work other biceps.

Negative-Only Chin-up on Multi-Exercise

1. Place cross bar in forward position.
2. Adjust carriage to proper height. When standing on top step, chin should be barely over bar.
3. Grasp cross bar with palms up.
4. Climb stairs.

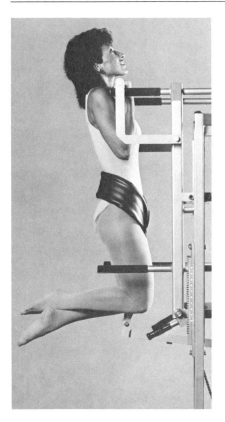

5. Place chin over bar and elbows by sides. Bend legs.

6. Lower body slowly (8–10 seconds).
7. Climb up and repeat.

Triceps Extension (Plateloading)

1. Adjust seat posi-
tion, with pads if
necessary, until
shoulders are on same
level as elbows.
2. Place elbows in
line with axis of cam
and hands with thumbs
up on pads.

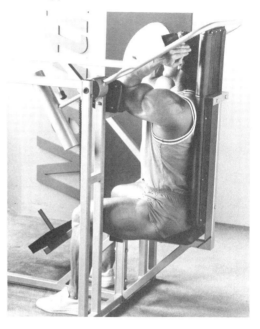

3. Straighten arms
smoothly.
4. Pause.
5. Return slowly to
stretched position.
6. Repeat.

Multi-Triceps Extension (Next Generation)

1. Adjust seat to level where elbows are slightly higher than shoulders when upper arms are resting on padded support in front of torso.

2. Position elbows on axes of rotation. Axes are marked with red dots.

3. Adjust seat back so elbows remain in proper alignment.

4. Place sides of hands against movement arm pads. Stabilize feet on floor and keep legs relaxed throughout exercise.

5. Move into a moderately stretched position in which hands are approximately across from ears.

6. Extend both arms simultaneously until elbows are straight.

7. Pause.

8. Lower slowly to moderate stretch.

9. Repeat.

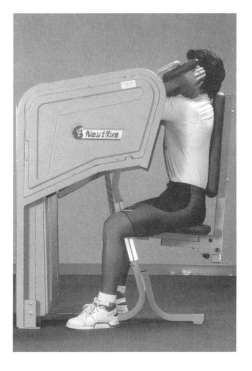 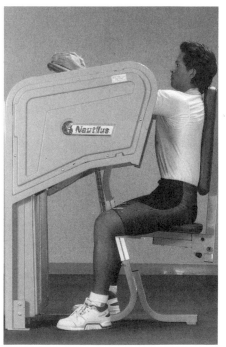

Negative-Only Dip on Multi-Exercise

1. Adjust carriage to proper level. It is important to allow ample stretch in bottom position.

2. Climb steps.

3. Lock elbows and bend knees.

4. Lower body slowly by bending arms (8–10 seconds).

5. Stretch at bottom position.

6. Climb up and repeat.

Seated Dip (Next Generation)

1. Sit in machine. Handles should be near armpits. If not, adjust seat bottom.
2. Fasten seat belt.
3. Place hands on top of handles.
4. Press handles downward until arms are almost straight.
5. Do not jam into forceful lockout.
6. Allow handles to rise slowly for stretch.
7. Repeat.

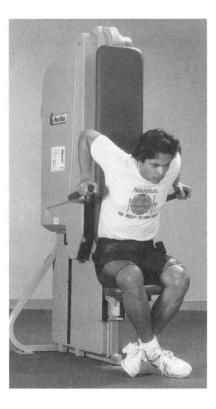 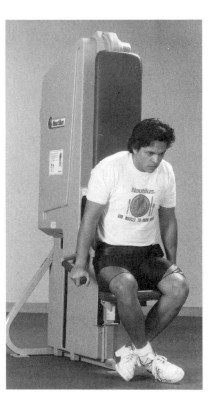

Triceps Extension with Towel on Multi-Exercise

1. Loop a lightweight towel through weight belt of multi-exercise machine.

2. Grasp one end of towel in each hand. Stand and face away from machine.

3. Adjust grip on towel until weight stack is separated.

4. Straighten arms in smooth fashion.

5. Pause.

6. Lower resistance slowly.

7. Repeat.

Wrist Curl on Multi-Exercise

1. Sit in front of multi-exercise machine, using chair, with toes under first step. Pad seat if necessary until hips are higher than knees.
2. Attach small bar to movement arm.
3. Grasp handles in palms-up fashion.
4. Place forearms firmly against thighs.

5. Lean forward to isolate forearm flexors. The angle between the upper arms and the forearms should be less than 90 degrees.
6. Curl small bar forward.
7. Pause.
8. Lower resistance slowly.
9. Repeat.

Reverse Wrist Curl on Multi-Exercise

1. Sit in front of multi-exercise machine, using chair, with toes under first step. Pad seat if necessary until hips are higher than knees.

2. Attach small handle directly to movement arm.

3. Grasp handles in palms-down fashion.

4. Place forearms firmly against thighs.

5. Reverse-curl small ball upward.

6. Pause.

7. Lower resistance slowly.

8. Repeat.

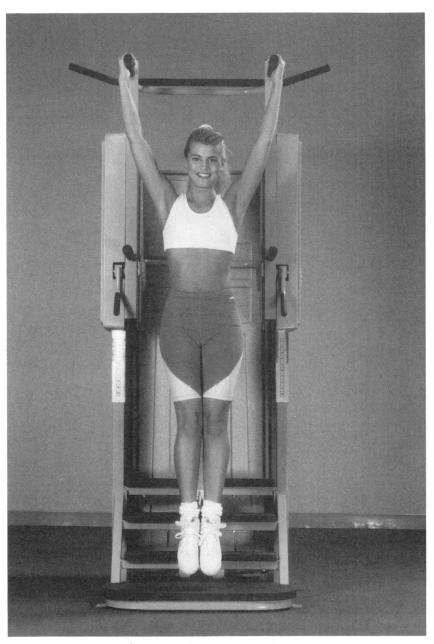

The Next Generation multi-exercise machine may be used for many movements, including the dip, chin-up, calf raise, and wrist curl.

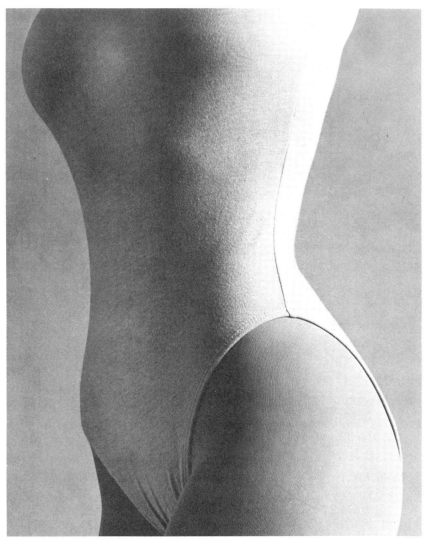

A trim waistline is a sign of vibrant health.

20
Waist

Few features stand out in a bathing suit as much as a slim, trim waistline. In clothes, a slender waist can make an individual's positive traits more alluring and the negative ones less noticeable.

A trim midsection makes the chest look fuller and the shoulders broader. A lean, muscular waist gives the individual a vibrant, athletic appearance.

Even more important than appearance is health. A soft, flabby belly is a good indication that too much fat surrounds the vital organs. Excessive body fat can overload the heart and lead to serious ailments.

MUSCLES OF THE WAIST

The appearance and strength of the waist are determined primarily by three muscles: rectus abdominis, external oblique, and internal oblique.

The rectus abdominis is attached to the fifth, sixth, and seventh ribs, extends across the front of the abdominal wall, and joins the pubis bone. Its primary function is to shorten the distance between the lower portion of the sternum and the pelvic girdle.

On both sides of the waist lie the external and internal obliques. The external oblique muscles attach to the lower ribs and extend around the outer waist until they join the hipbone. Their primary function is to bend the spine to the same side and to rotate the torso to the opposite side. The internal oblique is a sheath of muscle beneath the external oblique. The fibers run at right angles to those of the outer muscle. Lateral flexion to the same side and torso rotation to the same side are the main functions of the internal oblique muscles.

THE TRUTH ABOUT SIT-UPS AND LEG RAISES

The belief that sit-ups and leg raises are abdominal exercises is a misconception. These movements primarily work the hip flexors or iliopsoas muscles. The hip flexors connect the upper femur bones of the thighs to the lower lumbar region of the spine. When these muscles contract they pull the upper body to a sitting position; or they pull the thighs toward the chest, as in a leg raise. The rectus abdominis is only mildly involved in a traditional sit-up or leg raise.

The problem with the sit-up and leg raise has now been solved with the Nautilus abdominal machine. This new machine effectively isolates and works the rectus abdominis to a degree not possible with conventional exercises.

HIGH-REPETITION MISCONCEPTION

Another common misconception is that the midsection will be reduced if subjected to more repetitions than other body parts. Many people perform sit-ups and leg raises by the hundreds in a mistaken belief that they will assist in burning fat and defining the waistline. Exercise for the midsection has little effect on fat loss in the waist. It cannot be emphasized too often that spot reduction is not possible. The abdominals should be treated as any other muscle group. One set of 8–12 repetitions should be performed on the Nautilus abdominal machine, When 12 or more repetitions can be performed correctly resistance should be added.

High-repetition exercises have also been the rule in working the oblique muscles. Fitness-minded individuals often perform thousands of twisting movements with an empty bar to remove fatty deposits from their sides. Since the bar on the shoulders is being rotated horizontally, little resistance is ever applied to the external and internal obliques. The muscles are merely being stretched.

In the summer of 1981, after years of research, Nautilus introduced the rotary torso machine. It is the first device to provide effective, full-range exercise for the external and internal obliques. Like the abdominal machine, the rotary torso should be performed for only one set of 8–12 repetitions.

Abdominal I

1. Sit in machine.
2. Locate axis of rotation on right side.
3. Adjust seat so axis of rotation is at same level as lower ribs.
4. Place ankles behind roller pads.
5. Spread knees and sit erect.
6. Grasp handles.

7. Keep shoulders and head firmly against seat back.
8. Shorten distance between rib cage and navel by contracting abdominals only.
9. Keep legs relaxed and knees wide as seat bottom is elevated.
10. Pause in contracted position.
11. Return slowly to starting position.
12. Repeat.

Abdominal II

1. Sit in machine with swivel pads in front of chest.
2. Adjust seat until axis of rotation of movement arm is parallel to navel.

3. Hook both feet under bottom roller pads.
4. Adjust swivel pads on chest to comfortable position.
5. Place hands across waist.
6. Keep knees wide.

7. Move torso smoothly toward thighs.
8. Pause in contracted position.
9. Return slowly to starting position.
10. Repeat.

Abdominal (Next Generation)

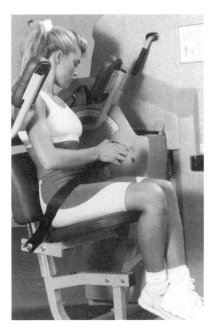

1. Adjust seat so navel aligns with red dot on side of machine.
2. Fasten seat belt across hips.

3. Place elbows on pads and grasp handles lightly.

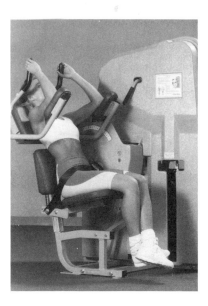

4. Pull with elbows and shorten distance between ribs and pelvis. Do not try to pivot around hips.

5. Pause in contracted position. Keep shoulders against seat back.

6. Return slowly to starting position.

7. Repeat.

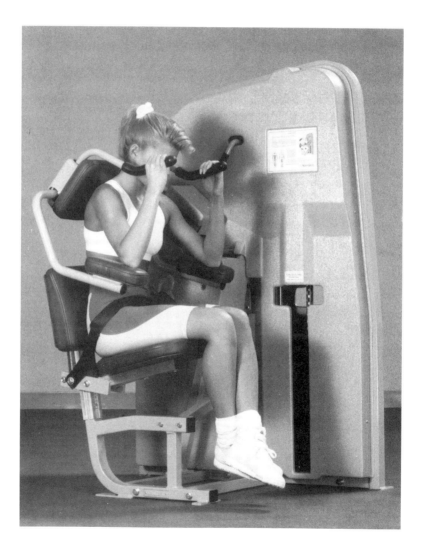

Rotary Torso (Next Generation)

1. Straddle seat. Make sure it is locked into extreme right or left position. Anchor lower body by crossing ankles.

2. Position head and spinal column directly above movement arm's pivot point.

3. Fasten seat belt across thighs.

4. Place upper arms securely over angled roller pads behind back. Elbows should be as close together as comfortably possible with hands up.

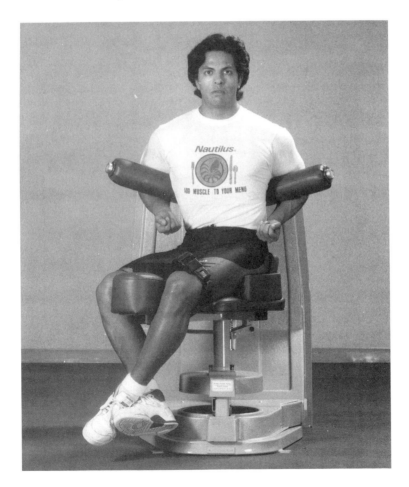

5. Allow back pressure of movement arm to rotate torso in one direction for moderate stretch.

6. Rotate smoothly to opposite side.

7. Pause.

8. Return to stretched position.

9. Repeat.

10. Adjust seat to opposite side and work other side.

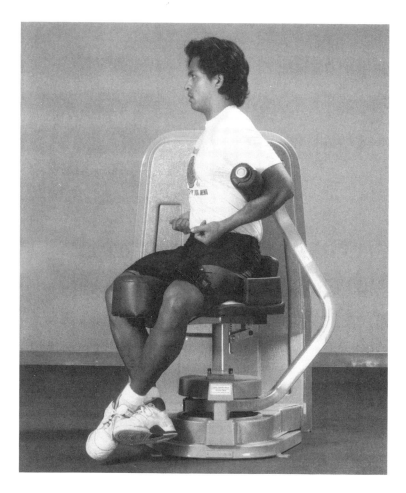

Side Bend on Multi-Exercise

1. Attach belt or handle to movement arm of multi-exercise machine.
2. Grasp handles in left hand with left shoulder facing machine.
3. Assume a standing position.
4. Place right hand on top of head.

5. Bend to left side.
6. Return to standing position.
7. Repeat.

8. Change hand and do side bend to right side.

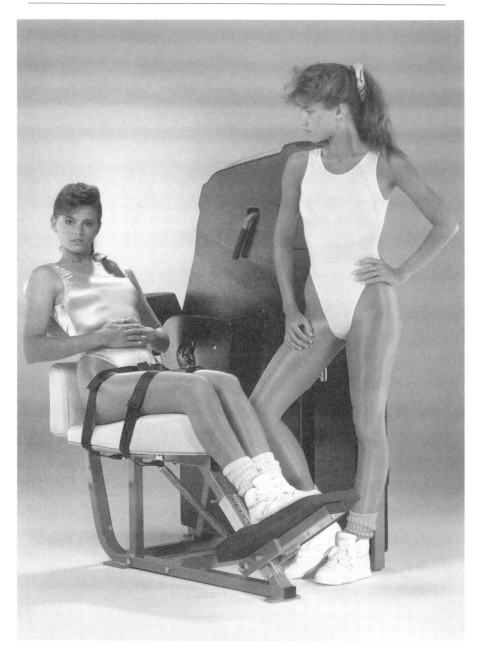

The Next Generation lower back machine works the erector spinae
muscles without compressing the spine.

21
Lower Back

Lower-back pain takes a backseat only to headache as the most common medical complaint. Backache is second only to the common cold as a reason for missed work. Odds are 10 to 1 that eventually you will suffer from lower-back pain.

According to medical expert Dr. Hans Kraus of the New York University College of Medicine, 80 percent of all lower back problems are the result of muscle weakness or tightness in one or more of the key muscle groups that support and control the movement of the spinal column. It is the lack of strength in these muscles, caused by inadequate or incorrect physical activity, that predisposes the back to both major and minor strains.

An examination of the spinal column and its support mechanism will help to clarify the problem of back pain.

ANATOMY OF THE SPINE

The spine stretches from the head to the buttocks. Starting from the head, it consists of 7 neck vertebrae, 12 dorsal vertebrae in the middle of the back, 5 lumbar vertebrae in the small of the back, and the sacrum, a triangular-shaped bone that connects the spinal column with the pelvis.

The vertebrae are not linked directly to one another. They are separated by ligamentous rings with a soft inner part, like a jelly doughnut. These rings are known as *discs.*

Besides the discs, there are strong ligaments joining the vertebral bodies with one another and with the sacrum. On the back part of each vertebra is a bony ring. This holds the spinal cord. The center of this cord consists of nerve cells. Surrounding it are large cables of nerve fibers that ultimately join the lower and upper parts of the body. The nerve cables contain all the connections to the muscles and help conduct the reflexes. These nerves, traveling through their cable links, transmit orders from the brain and the spinal cord to make muscles contract.

The normal spinal column is formed in the shape of a gentle S. The ligaments and discs together make the spinal column an elastic structure. But to function correctly to offset sudden blows and bear strain, the spinal column needs help. This help is given by the muscles.

Numerous muscles directly or indirectly lend support to the spine. The erector spinae muscles, abdominal muscles, hip flexors, hip extensors, neck muscles, and even the thigh muscles support the spinal column. They combine to keep it erect and allow it to move. They also protect the spine by acting as an outer guard.

When people complain of low back pain, they usually blame the spinal erector muscles. The spinal erectors are a series of long, deep muscles that extend from the sacrum to the skull on both sides of the spine. When these muscles contract they extend the spine backward.

Barbell exercises for the spinal erectors primarily involve lifting and lowering heavy weights to the waist and shoulders. The two most popular movements are the deadlift and the power clean. Both provide exercise for the spinal erectors, but the resistance does not vary in proportion to the potential strength of the involved muscles. Furthermore, because of the fast, jerky lifting techniques that are usually adhered to in performing these exercises, tremendous compression forces are exerted on the spine. Such compression forces cause many more injuries than they cure.

Yet strengthening your spinal erector muscles requires force—force within reasonable limits without unnecessary compression. With a barbell this is impossible. Nautilus, however, solved this problem in 1982 with the introduction of the lower back machine.

MOST IMPORTANT MACHINE

Arthur Jones believes that the Nautilus lower back machine is the most important machine he has ever produced. Why? Because the lower back machine eliminates compression forces on the spine as it moves through its entire range of motion. The resistance on the movement arm is always perpendicular to your spinal column. It strengthens your lower back without dangerous vertical loading.

The Nautilus lower back machine should be used in conjunction with the abdominal, hip and back, hip flexion, and rotary torso machines to build a strong girdle of muscle around the lumbar spine. Such strengthening will be a long step in the direction of making your lower back a dynamic ally instead of a nagging problem.

Lower Back

1. Enter machine from side by straddling seat.

2. Sit on seat bottom, not angle between seat bottom and seat back. Upper back should be underneath highest roller pad.

3. Stabilize lower body by moving thighs under bottom roller pads.

4. Place feet firmly on platform.

5. Fasten seat belt around hips.

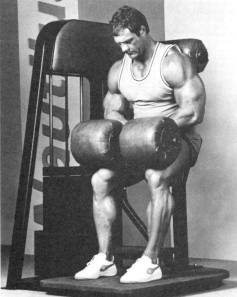

6. Interlace fingers across waist.

7. Move torso smoothly backward until in line with thighs.
8. Pause in contracted position.
9. Return slowly to starting position.
10. Repeat.

Lower Back (Next Generation)

1. Sit in machine. Make sure hips are well back in seat.
2. Adjust footrest so legs are slightly elevated off seat bottom. Some small individuals may require an extra pad to sit on.
3. Fasten seat belts securely across hips and thighs.

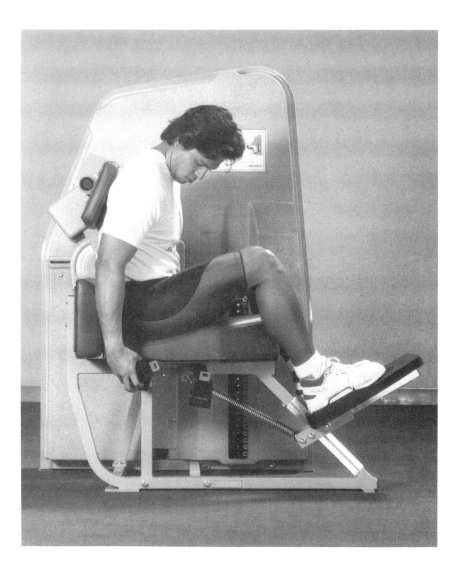

4. Interlace fingers across waist.

5. Extend torso backward by rotating around lumbar spine.

6. Pause in contracted position.

7. Return slowly to starting position.

8. Repeat.

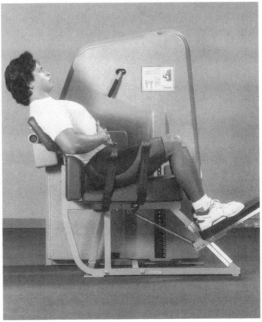

Direct exercise for the neck muscles is supplied by the 4-way neck machine.

22
Neck

No part of the body is taken for granted as much as the neck, but few muscles are more important.

The neck acts as a natural barometer for the body. Illness shows its effect by giving the neck a haggard, drawn look. The healthy person has fullness of neck that adds confidence to his appearance.

Football players, wrestlers, boxers, and other athletes know the importance of a powerful neck. It acts as a shock absorber, preventing injury to the head, shoulders, and neck itself. The neck enables the athlete to use his head physically as well as mentally. Strong neck muscles permit such violent actions as blocking and tackling in football and bridging in wrestling. Athletes have survived serious automobile accidents because of the strength and development of their necks.

Whiplash and other neck injuries befall thousands of people every week as a result of minor accidents. Many of these injuries would not have happened if the victim had had a strong neck. Even in simple calisthenic-type exercises or weekend sporting activities there are many cases of preventable stiff necks and pulled neck muscles.

A strong neck is not only a safeguard against injury but also an addition to personal appearance. A thin, scrawny neck stands out conspicuously even in the best-built man or woman.

In bodybuilding magazines some so-called experts advise against neck work. They reason that a large neck will detract from shoulder width. This makes about as much sense as never working the lower body so the upper body will look bigger. One of the real values of bodybuilding comes from all-over symmetry, from the pleasing development of all major muscle groups. Fortunately, for those who want to strengthen the neck, that part of the body responds quickly to proper exercise.

When they are provided with direct exercise the muscles of the neck are perhaps the easiest in the body to develop. Until the advent of the Nautilus neck machines, there was no practical method of providing such direct exercise. Most of the available exercises were clumsy, difficult to perform, uncomfortable, and sometimes even dangerous. As a result, this important section of the body has been largely ignored.

ANATOMY OF THE NECK

When man assumed the upright position, the huge muscles of the nape of the neck atrophied. Now man balances his head, weighing about 14 pounds, on 7 small cervical vertebrae. The only restraining elements that oppose sudden movements of the neck are the strength and integrity of the cervical vertebrae, the spinal ligaments, and the neck muscles. It is essential, therefore, to strengthen and develop this protective musculature.

At least 15 small and medium-sized muscles make up the majority of the neck's mass. These muscles are capable of producing movement in 7 different directions:

1. Elevating the shoulders
2. Bending the head toward the chest
3. Drawing the head backward
4. Bending the head down toward the right shoulder
5. Bending the head down toward the left shoulder
6. Twisting the head to look over the right shoulder
7. Twisting the head to look over the left shoulder

When full-range exercise is provided for those seven functions, the response of the neck muscles is immediate. The neck responds quickly to exercise because its muscles are exposed to so little hard work. Development of the neck muscles, therefore, is not a matter of years but of weeks.

4-Way Neck (Next Generation)

Adjust seat so while sitting erect your throat is on same level as axis of rotation of movement arm. Axis is marked with a red dot. This seat position will be correct for all four movements.

Back Extension

1. Enter machine with back of head against center of pad.
2. Stabilize torso by grasping handles lightly.

3. Push pad upward while straightening spine and raising chest.
4. Continue pushing pad backward while moving shoulders forward.
5. Extend neck as far back as comfortably possible.
6. Pause.
7. Return smoothly to starting position.
8. Repeat.

Front Flexion

1. Enter machine with face firmly against center of pad.
2. Stabilize torso by grasping handles lightly.
3. Move head backward slowly to extended position.

4. Push face forward carefully. Keep chest raised till pad touches chest.
5. Pause.
6. Return smoothly to starting position.
7. Repeat.

Lateral Contraction

1. Enter machine with right ear against center of pad.
2. Stabilize torso by grasping handles lightly.

3. Move head toward right shoulder.
4. Pause.
5. Keep shoulders square.
6. Return smoothly to starting position.
7. Repeat.
8. Enter machine from opposite direction and perform lateral contraction to left.

Rotary Neck

1. Sit facing away from machine.

2. Move head between pads.

3. Adjust head pads to a snug position by pulling overhead lever from right to left.

4. Push the hand levers to provide the resistance. Negative-only exercise can be provided by pressure on either hand lever, which will force the head to turn. This turning pressure is resisted by the neck muscles.

5. Push with the right hand lever, or pull with the left hand lever, to force the neck and head to rotate to the left or vice versa.

6. Perform six negative-only repetitions to the right and six negative-only repetitions to the left in an alternate fashion.

7. Release the head pads by pulling overhead lever from left to right.

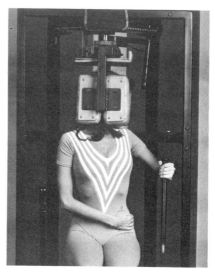

Neck and Shoulder

1. Place forearms between pads while seated.

2. Keep palms open and back of hands pressed against bottom pads.

3. Straighten torso until weight stack is lifted. Seat may be raised with elevation pads.

4. Elevate shoulders smoothly as high as possible. Keep elbows by sides when shrugging. Do not lean back.

5. Pause.

6. Return slowly to stretched position.

7. Repeat.

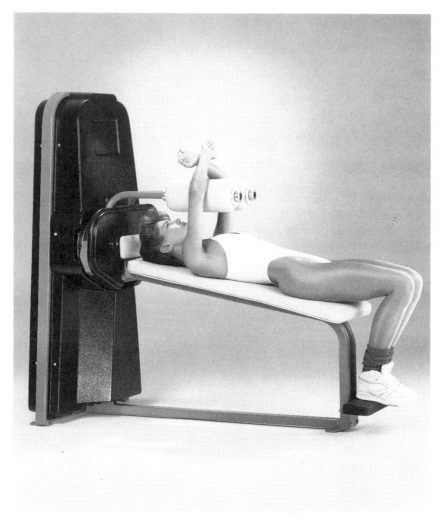

One of the most productive exercises for the pectoralis major muscles is the 10° chest.

23

Nautilus Routines

The following master list of exercises, grouped by body part and equipment, is a summation of the last nine chapters.

Forty-nine machines or exercises are listed. Trying to include most of them in the same workout would be a big mistake. Remember, it's the quality, not the quantity, of exercise that's most important.

MASTER LISTING OF EXERCISES

Body Part	Nautilus Machine or Exercise
Hips	Duo Hip and Back
	Hip Abduction
	Hip Flexion*
Legs	Leg Extension
	Leg Press
	Duo Squat
	Duo Leg Press
	Leg Curl
	Hip Adduction
	Calf Raise on Multi-Exercise

* Hip Flexion could also be placed in waist section.

Back	Pullover
	Women's Pullover
	Behind Neck
	Behind Neck Pulldown on Torso Arm
	Compound Rowing
Shoulders	Lateral Raise
	Overhead Press
	Double Shoulder Lateral Raise
	Double Shoulder Overhead Press
	Rowing Torso
	70° Shoulder
	Reverse Pullover
Chest	Men's Chest
	Women's Chest
	Double Chest Arm Cross
	Double Chest Decline Press
	Duo Decline Press
	Bench Press
	10° Chest
	40° Chest/Shoulder or 50° Chest/Shoulder
Arms	Biceps Curl (Plateloading)
	Multi-Biceps Curl
	Compound Position Biceps
	Chin-Up on Multi-Exercise
	Triceps Extension (Plateloading)
	Multi-Triceps Extension
	Dip on Multi-Exercise
	Seated Dip
	Triceps Extension with Towel on Multi-Exercise
	Wrist Curl on Multi-Exercise
	Reverse Wrist Curl on Multi-Exercise
Waist	Abdominal
	Rotary Torso
	Side Bend on Multi-Exercise
Lower Back	Lower Back
Neck	4-Way Neck
	Rotary Neck
	Neck and Shoulder

Organize your program using the Nautilus training principles discussed in Chapter 7. Rule 1, for example, tells you to perform one set of 4–6 exercises for the lower body and 6–8 exercises for the upper body, and no more than 12 exercises in any workout.

A GRADUAL INTRODUCTION

If you are a beginner, you should undergo a two-week introduction to Nautilus equipment. Rather than performing 12 exercises, you are advised to begin with only 5 simple machines. A good choice would be leg extension, leg curl, pullover, decline press, and behind neck pulldown. Practice good form on each repetition.

After several learning sessions, you may add one or two new machines during each workout until all 12 exercises of Basic Nautilus Workout I are being utilized.

AFTER THE FIRST WEEK

The duo hip and back is often a difficult machine for a beginner to use. It should be introduced after the leg extension, leg curl, hip abduction, and hip adduction are mastered.

The overhead press on the double shoulder machine, because of its difficulty, should be initiated after you are skilled in the lateral raise.

The 4-way neck, since it provides exercise for the vulnerable cervical area of the spine, should be introduced last.

TRIED-AND-PROVEN ROUTINES

The following routines have been used successfully with men and women of all ages. If certain Nautilus machines are not available, substitutions can be made.

I

Basic Nautilus Workout

1. Duo Hip and Back
2. Hip Adduction
3. Leg Extension
4. Leg Curl
5. Pullover
6. Behind Neck Pulldown
7. Lateral Raise
8. Overhead Press
9. Neck and Shoulder
10. Arm Cross
11. Decline Press
12. 4-Way Neck

II

Basic Nautilus Workout

1. Hip Abduction
2. Leg Extension
3. Leg Press or Duo Squat
4. Calf Raise
5. Behind Neck
6. Behind Neck Pulldown
7. Dip
8. Rowing Torso
9. Multi-Triceps Extension
10. Multi-Biceps Curl
11. Abdominal
12. Lower Back

III

Basic Nautilus Workout

1. Side Leg Curl
2. Hip Adduction
3. Leg Press or Duo Squat
4. Hip Flexion
5. Pullover
6. Overhead Press
7. Chin or Negative Chin
8. Dip or Negative Dip
9. Wrist Curl
10. Reverse Wrist Curl
11. Abdominal
12. Rotary Torso

IV

Basic Nautilus Workout

1. Hip Flexion
2. Leg Extension
3. Leg Press or Duo Squat
4. Leg Curl
5. Calf Raise
6. Lateral Raise
7. Overhead Press
8. Pullover
9. Behind Neck Pulldown
10. Arm Cross
11. Decline Press
12. Neck and Shoulder

Note: In any applicable routine, you may substitute the following new machines: duo leg press for leg press, bench press for decline press or duo decline press, compound rowing for behind neck pulldown, seated dip for dip, 50° chest/shoulder for 40° chest/shoulder, and reverse pullover for lateral raise.

V

Basic Nautilus Workout

1. Hip Adduction
2. Hip Abduction
3. Duo Hip and Back
4. Hip Flexion
5. Behind Neck
6. 70° Shoulder
7. Decline Press
8. 10° Chest
9. Triceps Extension
10. Compound Position Biceps
11. Abdominal
12. Lower Back

VI

Basic Nautilus Workout

1. Leg Press or Duo Squat
2. Leg Extension
3. Calf Raise
4. Leg Curl
5. 40° Chest/Shoulder
6. Lateral Raise
7. Pullover
8. Duo Decline Press
9. Wrist Curl
10. Reverse Wrist Curl
11. 4-Way Neck
12. Rotary Neck

VII

Negative Nautilus Workout

1. Leg Extension (NA)
2. Leg Press (NA)
3. Leg Curl (NA)
4. Hip Adduction (NE)
5. Pullover (NO)
6. Chin (NO)
7. Lateral Raise (NO)
8. Overhead Press (NO)
9. Neck and Shoulder (NE)
10. Dip (NO)

VIII

Negative Nautilus Workout

1. Hip Abduction (NE)
2. Leg Curl (NE)
3. Leg Press (NE)
4. Leg Extension (NE)
5. Rowing Torso (NE)
6. Decline Press (NO)
7. Pullover (NA)
8. Overhead Press (NA)
9. Abdominal (NO)
10. 4-Way Neck (NO)

(NO)—Negative-only exercise: the positive portion of an exercise movement is performed by assistants, or by the trainee's legs, as a heavier-than-normal weight is slowly lowered by the trainee.

(NA)—Negative-accentuated exercise: the trainee lifts the resistance with two limbs and slowly lowers with one limb.

(NE)—Negative-emphasized exercise: a lighter-than-normal weight is used on the positive part of the movement. Additional resistance is then provided in the negative phase by an assistant's pressing down on the weight stack.

	IX	X
	Nautilus Preexhaustion Workout	*Nautilus Preexhaustion Workout*

IX	X
1. Leg Curl	1. Leg Curl
2. Hip Adduction	2. Leg Extension
3. Hip and Back	3. Leg Press
4. Leg Extension	4. Behind Neck Pulldown
5. Leg Press	5. Behind Neck
6. Pullover	6. Chin (NO)
7. Behind Neck	7. Decline Press
8. Behind Neck Pulldown	8. Arm Cross
9. Triceps Extension with Towel	9. Dip (NO)
10. Dip (NO)	10. Hip Flexion
11. Biceps Curl	11. Abdominal
12. Chin (NO)	12. Pullover

In Preexhaustion Workouts IX and X, rest only between exercises separated by a rule.

XI

*Nautilus Push-and-Pull
Workout*

1. Hip Abduction
2. Hip Adduction
3. Leg Extension
4. Leg Curl
5. Overhead Press
6. Chin
7. Decline Press
8. Behind Neck Pulldown
9. Dip
10. Pullover
11. Multi-Triceps Extension
12. Multi-Biceps Curl

XII

*Nautilus Push-and-Pull
Workout*

1. Duo Hip and Back
2. Hip Flexion
3. Leg Curl
4. Duo Squat
5. 10° Chest
6. Rowing Torso
7. Behind Neck
8. 70° Shoulder
9. Neck and Shoulder
10. Lower Back
11. Side Bend
12. 4-Way Neck

XIII

*Nautilus Change-of-Pace
Workout*

1. Overhead Press
2. Chin
3. Duo Decline Press
4. Pullover
5. Dip
6. Rowing Torso
7. Leg Extension
8. Leg Curl
9. Triceps Extension with
   Towel
10. Compound Position Biceps
11. Hip Flexion

XIV

*Nautilus Change-of-Pace
Workout*

1. Leg Press (Seat Back)
2. Pullover
3. Leg Press (Seat Close)
4. Behind Neck
5. Calf Raise
6. Abdominal
7. Dip
8. Triceps Extension
9. Chin
10. Biceps Curl
11. Lower Back

IMPORTANT NOTE

Individuals who train on Nautilus equipment in commercial fitness centers should make certain that they have the management's approval before any listed routine is tried. Under some circumstances it is neither practical nor advisable to perform certain exercises or routines.

CHOOSING A ROUTINE

Most people should start with Basic Nautilus Workout I. This workout should be performed three times a week for one or two months, or until you master or feel confident with each exercise. You may then start alternating I with II, III, IV, V, and VI. After four more months you should perform one negative workout per week. The other two workouts should come from the basic group. After several months of negative workouts any of the other workouts can be used.

SPECIAL CONSIDERATIONS

Sports Routines

How do you design a Nautilus routine for a specific sport? First, you need to examine your activity closely. Which parts of your body are used most? Running, jumping, and kicking involve the hips, thighs, and calves. Throwing and catching use the torso and arms. Bending over brings into action the lower back.

Most sports require high levels of strength and conditioning in all major body parts and muscle groups. There are, however, a few exceptions. Swimming and gymnastics emphasize the upper body more than the lower body. Long-distance running and soccer involve the lower body more than the upper body.

Once you determine the body parts that need to be strengthened, the next step is to select Nautilus exercises that involve those body parts. Below are examples of suggested routines for four popular sports.

Nautilus Football Routine

Body parts to emphasize: hips, thighs, shoulders, arms, lower back, and neck.

1. Duo Hip and Back
2. Leg Extension
3. Leg Curl
4. Duo Squat
5. Lateral Raise
6. Overhead Press
7. Pullover
8. Multi-Triceps Extension
9. Multi-Biceps Curl
10. Lower Back
11. 4-Way Neck
12. Neck and Shoulder

Nautilus Swimming Routine

Body parts to emphasize: hips, thighs, back, chest, shoulders, arms, and lower back.

1. Hip Adduction
2. Hip Abduction
3. Leg Curl
4. Leg Extension
5. Behind Neck
6. 40° Chest/Shoulder
7. Pullover
8. 10° Chest

9. Rowing Torso
10. Multi-Triceps Extension
11. Multi-Biceps Curl
12. Lower Back

Nautilus Tennis Routine

Body parts to emphasize: hips, thighs, calves, shoulders, chest, back, arms, forearms, and waist.

1. Hip Adduction
2. Leg Curl
3. Leg Extension
4. Calf Raise
5. Lateral Raise
6. Pullover
7. 10° Chest
8. Multi-Biceps Curl
9. Multi-Triceps Extension
10. Wrist Curl
11. Reverse Wrist Curl
12. Rotary Torso

Nautilus Running Routine

Body parts to emphasize: hips, thighs, calves, back, shoulders, waist, and lower back.

1. Duo Hip and Back
2. Hip Flexion
3. Leg Extension
4. Leg Curl
5. Calf Raise
6. Hip Adduction
7. Pullover
8. Behind Neck Pulldown

   9. Arm Cross
  10. Neck and Shoulder
  11. Abdominal
  12. Lower Back

It is a mistake to assume that the stronger athletes become, the more exercise they need. You should never perform more than 12 exercises in any one workout. For many advanced, stronger athletes, the total number of exercises must be reduced to 10, or even to 8. Nautilus sessions should not be performed more than 3 times a week. Even this number may have to be reduced.

In-season Nautilus training for an athlete merits special consideration. Too many athletes make the mistake of developing high levels of strength during the off-season and gradually losing strength during the season. To increase or even maintain muscular strength during the season, athletes must train hard at least once every four days. Steady progress can be made on a twice-a-week program.

Most in-season Nautilus training should be limited to twice a week. Usually the athletes who play a significant role during the game are trained the next day and again three days later. Training the day following the game eliminates much of the after-game soreness. The athletes who get little or no playing time during the game should continue training hard three times a week.

Specialized Routines for Women

Generally speaking, women have the same kind and number of muscles as men. The only difference between the training of men and women involves the amount of resistance on the machine. Women will usually handle less weight than men. The training principles and program organization should be basically the same for women as for men.

There are, however, some exceptions.

Some women have an area of the body—such as the hips, thighs, chest, or waist—that merits special attention. If you have a problem area, then the routines below may offer a solution.

Specialized Hip Routine

1. Hip Abduction
2. Duo Hip and Back
3. Hip Flexion
4. Duo Squat or Leg Press
5. Leg Curl
6. Leg Extension
7. Lower Back
8. Pullover or Women's Pullover
9. Lateral Raise
10. Behind Neck Pulldown
11. Decline Press
12. Hip Abduction

Specialized Thigh Routine

1. Leg Extension
2. Leg Press or Duo Squat
3. Leg Curl
4. Hip Abduction
5. Hip Adduction
6. Hip Flexion
7. Pullover or Women's Pullover
8. Behind Neck Pulldown
9. Arm Cross
10. Decline Press
11. Leg Extension
12. Leg Curl

Specialized Chest Routine

1. Arm Cross or Women's Chest
2. Decline Press
3. Pullover or Women's Pullover
4. 40° Chest/Shoulder
5. Rowing Torso
6. Lateral Raise
7. Behind Neck Pulldown
8. Leg Extension
9. Leg Curl
10. Calf Raise
11. Abdominal
12. Decline Press

Specialized Waist Routine

1. Hip Flexion
2. Abdominal
3. Rotary Torso
4. Duo Hip and Back
5. Pullover or Women's Pulldown
6. Overhead Press
7. Arm Cross or Women's Chest
8. Leg Extension
9. Leg Curl
10. Duo Squat
11. Hip Flexion
12. Abdominal

Most of the specialized routines are composed of seven exercises for the problem area and five exercises for the rest of your body. One of the best exercises for the problem body part is usually done for two sets. Frequently, the best exercise is performed first and last in the routine.

Doing two sets of a Nautilus exercise in the same workout is seldom a proficient way to shape and strengthen the body. But by performing the same exercise first and last in the routine, a slightly different degree of muscle-fiber recruitment is involved. This seems to stimulate additional firming and toning in the problem area.

An important concept to understand in using the specialized Nautilus programs is that the body will tolerate only a limited amount of disproportionate training. Women who want to strengthen and shape the thighs, for example, will accomplish this more efficiently by training all the major parts of the body, not just the thighs. From this standpoint, a specialized routine should not be used more than twice a week.

A specialized routine might be performed on Monday and Friday of a given week. But one of the basic routines should be practiced on Wednesday.

A woman with several problem areas, such as the hips and waist, might perform a specialized routine for the hips on Monday, a specialized routine for the waist on Wednesday, and a basic routine for the entire body on Friday. Regardless of the number of problem areas that a woman may have, she should always adhere to at least one basic workout per week. This will assure the best possible body-shaping results.

What Works for One Successful Fitness Center

At the Gainesville Health and Fitness Center in Gainesville, Florida, we train more than 900 people a day in our Nautilus program. Sometimes we have as many as 30 new members per day. To train this number of old and new members successfully requires 5 lines of Nautilus equipment. In addition, it requires well-organized procedures and dedicated instructors.

When a person first enrolls, he or she is given a packet containing club policies, Nautilus equipment information, and a variety of articles about fitness. Every two weeks we hold a "get-acquainted session" for the new members. Other members are invited to attend as well. The session lasts one hour and includes a brief presentation followed by questions and answers.

Joe Cirulli's Gainesville Health and Fitness Club has 57 Nautilus machines in its exercise area. (Photo by Susan Cunningham)

The beginning workout consists of only 5 exercises. Every other workout, a new exercise is added. Within 4 weeks our new members are performing a full workout of 12 exercises. They seem to learn the correct form more efficiently in this gradual manner.

Every member must keep a workout card. The cards are

boxed on a long countertop in alphabetical order according to the members' last names. The beginning card is colored green, and there is space for 12 sessions. The first 12 workouts are basically the same for everybody.

After 12 workouts, or approximately 4 weeks, the member progresses to another workout card. The first card is placed in his permanent folder and filed for safekeeping. Other completed cards will be filed as well. The second card consists of a variety of different routines.

We've found that most people like the variety of exercises that they use during the second month. Variety helps them maintain their enthusiasm. Our second cards are also color-coded, as are our third, fourth, and fifth cards. Color-coding enables an instructor to see at a glance what point a member has reached in the overall program. This helps our instructors use their time more efficiently.

The third workout card lists all the Nautilus machines and exercises in our center. During this month the members are encouraged to design, with the help of an instructor, their own routines, using the 12 Nautilus rules as guidelines. Members can, however, continue to use the routines from card 1 or 2.

The fourth progression employs a card that concentrates on specialized routines: routines for the hips, thighs, waist, back, chest, and arms. These routines were taken from Dr. Darden's books and are listed on the wall in the middle of the workout area. The exercise sequence, no matter which routine is followed, is in accordance with the order of our machines. This greatly facilitates the traffic flow. Most of the machines are arranged from larger to smaller muscle groups.

After four months of supervised training the majority of our members feel very confident in organizing their own Nautilus routines. They receive a fifth card, again in a different color. But it's still our policy to have several skilled instructors on the floor at all times to assist all advanced members with their routines and exercises.

Joe Cirulli

Routines for the 10–14 Age Group

Muscular strength is an important factor for the 10–14 age group for several reasons. First, strength provides the power behind all bodily movement. Second, it plays an important role in protecting the young from injury. Stronger muscles, of course, increase strength and joint stability.

A properly conducted Nautilus training program produces the following results for the 10–14 age group:

1. Increased muscular strength
2. Stronger ligaments, tendons, and connective tissues
3. Improved flexibility
4. Stronger bones
5. Increased heart-lung efficiency
6. Better protection against injury
7. Improved coordination
8. Faster speed of movement

Nautilus training of both boys and girls before puberty, and girls after puberty, produces little muscular development. The dominant masculinizing hormone, testosterone, is not secreted in large enough amounts in women to affect growth. Large muscular size from exercise, therefore, is possible after puberty only in males.

Prior to the age of about 10, most children will profit more by learning and practicing basic movement skills such as throwing, kicking, tumbling, climbing, jumping, and swinging. After the age of 10, however, properly conducted Nautilus training will benefit all children.

Basically, the same Nautilus training principles that have been used successfully with mature athletes apply to the 10–14 age group. It is very important that the young pay attention to good form in all exercises. For them, supervision is absolutely necessary.

Children under five feet in height will have problems fitting into most Nautilus machines. They should build a basic level of strength with free-hand exercises before progressing to Nautilus machines. The following free-hand routine is recommended as a starter program.

1. Squat
2. Reverse Leg Raise
3. Calf Raise
4. Chin
5. Push-Up
6. Side Bend
7. Dip
8. Trunk Curl
9. Hand Resistance against Neck

Many Nautilus machines can be used by children. Special attention should be given to slow, smooth movements. Here, a behind neck pulldown is being performed by a 10-year-old girl. (Photo by Inge Cook)

The young should start out by performing eight repetitions of each exercise in good form. If that seems impossible on some movements, especially the chin, dip, or even the push-up, the following variations may be made.

In the chin an adolescent can use his legs to help get his chin over the bar. Place a wooden box in front of the chinning bar. Have him step on the box and put his chin over the bar. Have him remove his feet and lower himself very slowly, in six to eight seconds, then climb back and repeat. This is excellent exercise for the arms and back muscles. For building muscular strength, the lowering portion of the exercise is far more important than the rising part.

Dips on the parallel bars can be done in a similar manner. Have the boys and girls climb up, lock their arms, and lower themselves very slowly. This exercise works the chest, shoulders, and triceps.

In push-ups adolescents can use their knees and lower back to help straighten their arms. They should then slowly bend their arms until they touch the floor.

The squat can be done in one of two ways. Have the students bend their legs very slowly and smoothly, then stand up and repeat. They can work up to 10–15 seconds' lowering time on this exercise. Or have them lower themselves on one leg, stand up on two legs, and lower themselves on the opposite leg. Some may need a chair to hold on to for balance. For best results from these movements, only one set of 8–12 repetitions three times a week should be done.

Over-65 Age Group

The Census Bureau has estimated that 25 million people living in the United States are over the age of 65. If present birth trends continue, an estimated 20 percent of the population will be 65 and older by the year 2030. The percentage is now 10.5. By 2030 more than 64 million Americans will be 65 years old or older.

Physical fitness can certainly improve life for those over 65. For those with normal health there is no better exercise than Nautilus training.

There are a few people in this age group, however, who should avoid vigorous exercise. Exercise may aggravate the

George Peterson, who was 73 in 1984, and his wife Pat, who was 72, have been training on Nautilus equipment at the Athletic Center of Atlanta, Georgia, for over 10 years. When George started the program, he weighed 214 pounds and had a 43½-inch waist. Two years later, he weighed 192 pounds and his waist measured 37 inches. Today he still maintains those measurements. (Photo by Ellington Darden)

condition of those who have acute arthritis, anemia, tuberculosis, severe kidney or liver diseases, or severe heart problems. In these cases a physician's recommendations should be adhered to rigidly.

A complete medical examination should, of course, be a prerequisite for anyone over 65 who is interested in exercise.

A month of supervised free-hand exercises such as those described for adolescents would be appropriate to accustom sedentary muscles to progressive exercise. A Nautilus program could then be initiated with particular emphasis placed on slow, smooth, full-range movements. Results are often dramatic and very rewarding.

NAUTILUS FOR EVERYBODY

There is no age group that should be excluded from Nautilus exercise. It can enrich everybody's life. But it must be proper exercise—exercise properly organized, properly supervised, and properly performed.

The multi-triceps machine stretches and contracts the largest muscles of the upper arms.

24

Questions
and Answers

The best way to fill in gaps and clear up areas of confusion seems to be to use a simple question-and-answer format. The following are answers to questions frequently asked in seminar sessions and by visitors to Nautilus Sports/Medical Industries.

SELECTING STARTING WEIGHTS

Q. *As a beginning trainee, how do I determine the correct amount of weight to use on each Nautilus machine?*

A. Selecting the correct weight on a Nautilus machine comes from experience. But since you are a beginning trainee, you have no experience. The best thing to do, then, is to find an advanced trainee or a coach or an instructor who does have this experience and ask him or her.

The following starting weights are based on my experience

in training several thousand people. These starting weights apply best to people between the ages of 18 and 35. Please note that the lightest weight on any Nautilus machine is 20 pounds, which includes a single top plate and the vertical selector rod. Some machines have double top plates, so the lightest possible weight on them is 30 pounds. Each additional plate weighs 10 pounds.

The recommended starting weight on the arm cross for a beginning man is 50 pounds. The trainee above is using 80 pounds.

STARTING WEIGHTS FOR BEGINNERS
(in pounds)

Machine or Exercise	Men	Women
Duo Hip and Back	60	50
Hip Abduction	60	50
Hip Flexion	50	30
Leg Extension	70	50
Leg Press	70	60
Duo Squat	135	110
Leg Curl	50	40
Hip Adduction	70	50
Calf Raise	90	80
Pullover	70	30
Women's Pullover		80
Behind Neck	60	30
Behind Neck Pulldown	60	30

Machine or Exercise	Men	Women
Lateral Raise	60	30
Overhead Press	50	20
Double Shoulder Lateral Raise	50	20
Double Shoulder Overhead Press	30	20*
Rowing Torso	40	20
70° Shoulder	50	30
Women's Chest		40
Double Chest Arm Cross	50	20
Double Chest Decline Press	60	30
10° Chest	60	40
40° Chest/Shoulder	50	30
Biceps Curl (Plateloading)	25	10
Multi-Biceps Curl	50	20
Triceps Extension (Plateloading)	25	10

Multi-Triceps Extension	50	20
Wrist Curl	40	20
Reverse Wrist Curl	30	20
Abdominal	40	20
Rotary Torso	40	30
Lower Back	100	60
4-Way Neck	20	20*
Neck and Shoulder	30	20

*Perform this exercise in a negative-only manner.

STRENGTH RATINGS

Q. Do you have any norms or standards for determining how my strength on a Nautilus machine compares to other trainees?

A. No statistical norms or standards are available. But I can provide you with some figures I've used as goals for people I've trained personally. Please note that the "fair," "good," and "excellent" categories apply to the use of as much weight as possible for 10 continuous repetitions in correct form. The routines apply best to people in the 18–35 age group.

NAUTILUS STRENGTH RATINGS*
(in pounds for 10 repetitions)

Men	Fair	Good	Excellent
Leg Extension**	140 x 10	175 x 10	210 x 10
Leg Curl	85	105	130
Pullover	115	140	170
Behind Neck Pulldown	100	125	150
Double Chest, Arm Cross	100	125	150
Double Chest, Decline Press	115	145	180
Multi-Biceps	75	90	110
Multi-Triceps	80	95	115
Women	**Fair**	**Good**	**Excellent**
Leg Extension**	75 x 10	90 x 10	110 x 10
Leg Curl	55	65	80
Women's Pullover	115	140	170
Behind Neck Pulldown	55	70	85
Women's Chest	65	85	100
Double Chest, Decline Press	50	65	80
Multi-Biceps	40	50	60
Multi-Triceps	35	45	55

*No claims are made for the validity of these strength ratings. They are simply categories that have proved useful to the author in the past.
**Performed on the super leg extension machine with adjustable seat.

Sometimes a "superior" category is needed when you are training big, strong professional athletes. This goal could be established by taking 20 percent of the highest rating and adding it to the "excellent" poundage. For example, 20 percent of 210 pounds in the leg extension is 42. Forty-two plus 210 rounds off to 250 pounds. Thus, a superior rating for the leg extension would be 250 pounds for 10 repetitions.

TRAINING EXPECTATIONS

Q. *What can a typical man expect from a Nautilus program?*

A. Some physiologists say that the typical untrained man has the potential to increase his muscular strength by approxi-

Hypothetical example of changing exercise needs as strength increases. The weights given are averages of those used for all the exercises being done at a given time.

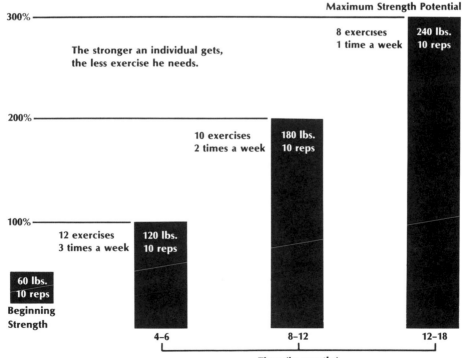

Maximum Strength Potential

300%

The stronger an individual gets,
the less exercise he needs.

8 exercises
1 time a week   240 lbs.
10 reps

200%

10 exercises
2 times a week   180 lbs.
10 reps

Percentage Strength Increase

100%

12 exercises
3 times a week   120 lbs.
10 reps

60 lbs.
10 reps
Beginning
Strength

4–6   8–12   12–18

Time (in months)

mately 300 percent. In reality, however, most men rarely get past the level of doubling their strength because they do not understand recovery ability.

Recovery ability has to do with the total chemical reactions that are necessary for your body to overcompensate and become bigger and stronger. Although the specifics of your recovery ability remain a mystery, it is recognized that these complex chemical interactions require time and rest. It is also known that your recovery ability does not increase in proportion to your capacity to get stronger.

While the typical man has the potential to increase his strength by 300 percent, he can only increase his recovery ability by about 50 percent. The stronger he becomes, the less exercise he needs.

Most trainees assume that, the stronger they get, the more exercise they need. But when they reach a certain level of strength they need shorter periods of harder exercise and longer periods of rest.

A hypothetical example should make this obvious. First, an individual's strength is tested to determine the amount of weight he can lift for 10 repetitions in 10 basic exercises. The results of this initial testing show he can do 60 pounds on the average for each exercise. Thus, his starting level is 60/10.

Assuming he trains properly, he can expect to double his strength in 4–6 months, triple his strength in 8–12 months, and quadruple his strength in 12–16 months.

It is possible for this individual to reach his potential strength level in 12–18 months if he trains properly and understands his recovery ability.

Initially, almost any type of Nautilus training program will produce increases in strength for several months, simply because it is harder work than the average man is used to doing. The average man, at first, is not strong enough to make very deep inroads into his recovery ability. There is a vast difference between the recovery period of a 60-pound strength level and that of a 120-pound strength level.

In progressing from the 60-pound level to the 120-pound level, you should perform about 12 exercises every other day, or three times per week. The 120-pound level is a critical point. Now you're strong enough to use up your recovery ability.

To progress to the 180-pound level, you're going to have to train less. You must reduce your exercises from 12 to 10 and reduce your hard training days from 3 times to 2 a week.

Further progression from the 180-pound level to the 240-pound level necessitates additional reductions from 10 exercises to 8 exercises and from 2 hard training days a week to one hard training day a week. The chart on page 275 summarizes these details.

FREQUENCY

Q. *After I double my strength, I should train only twice a week. Is that correct?*

A. You should still train three times a week, but only two of these workouts would be high-intensity. You would train hard on Mondays and Fridays and medium on Wednesdays. The medium workout consists of the same exercises and resistance as the hard workout, but the medium exercise is ended two or three repetitions sooner. The medium workout does not stimulate growth, but it does prevent strength losses. It does not use up as much of the trainee's recovery ability as a hard workout.

It should be obvious that the muscular structure cannot grow without recovery ability. No amount of stimulation will produce growth if the body cannot supply the requirements for that growth.

It is important to remember that the stronger you get, the less exercise you need.

POTENTIAL

Q. The chart on page 275 seems to indicate that if a trainee can perform 10 repetitions with 240 pounds on a certain exercise, he has reached his full potential. Is this correct?

A. No! The chart referred to a hypothetical example. In the chart, 240/10 represents the average of 10 different exercises after the trainee has quadrupled his strength. For example, using four Nautilus machines, he might be able to train with 150 pounds on the duo hip and back, 410 on the duo squat, 180 on the pullover, and 110 on the biceps curl. The average of these four exercises would be 212.5 pounds.

Naturally, an individual will be able to increase the strength of some muscle groups faster and to a greater degree than others. Much of this depends on his bodily proportions, neurological efficiency, and the size of the muscle mass that he is working.

The typical untrained man should be able to quadruple his overall strength, if he works out properly.

SUPERVISION

Q. What should I do when there is no instructor or coach available to supervise my training?

A. Find a training partner. You can then push each other one at a time through a hard workout. After several weeks of training, both partners should have learned enough about each other to organize productive training sessions.

PARTIAL REPETITIONS

Q. On a Nautilus machine, if I cannot complete a full range of movement after about eight repetitions, should I continue to do partial repetitions until failure?

A. The answer to this question depends on the Nautilus machine being used. On the single-joint rotary movements, such as the pullover, leg extension, and leg curl, the cams are about 90-percent efficient at working the desired muscle. Partial repetitions should not be done on the single-joint machines. Doing so places a disproportionate emphasis on part of the movement, since the cam is designed to work the muscle proportionately.

With the multiple-joint exercises, such as the leg press, overhead press, and pulldown, partial repetitions at the end of a set may be advantageous. Multiple-joint exercises on Nautilus machines are about 25-percent efficient. It is impossible to attain a proper full-range strength curve on such a movement, so partial repetitions are called for.

EXCESSIVE FACIAL EXPRESSION

Q. *What is so bad about "making faces" or excessive facial expression during Nautilus training?*

A. Any time you "make a face," you must contract many small muscles of the face and neck. Not only does this take a certain amount of energy, but it also reduces your ability to contract larger muscle groups repeatedly.

If you were trying to determine how much weight you could handle for a maximum-attempt, one-repetition effort, it might be beneficial to scream and shout and make faces. But unless you were a competitive weightlifter, there is no need to try to determine how much weight you can handle for one repetition.

In performing 8–12 repetitions of a dozen different exercises, making faces reduces your efficiency. If you are using the leg extension machine, you should concentrate on the quadriceps muscles as you perform the exercise, and at the same time try to relax the noninvolved muscles of your body. Bringing into play the facial or other upper body muscles forces your transport system to do a less efficient job on the legs.

Making faces convinces you, as well as your instructor, that you are working harder than you actually are. This reaction can stop you short of momentary muscular failure on many exercises.

Furthermore, making faces unnecessarily elevates the blood pressure. Forceful gripping of the hands also increases blood pressure to dangerously high levels. Since high-intensity exercise by itself elevates your blood pressure temporarily, there is no need to make it higher by making faces or by gripping excessively.

For better results from Nautilus exercise, you must learn to relax the muscles of your face, neck, and hands as well as other muscles that are not involved in the specific movement.

ABDOMINAL MACHINES

Q. *How does the Next Generation abdominal machine differ from previous ones?*

A. Nautilus has manufactured three versions of the abdominal machine. The first one was a crunch-type machine with a seat that raised as the movement progressed. Many people had difficulty using this version correctly. Instead of performing the movement with their abdominal muscles, they pulled with their arms.

The second abdominal machine removed the arms from the exercise. Swivel pads contacted the shoulders and upper chest. The exercise was performed by curling the trunk toward the hips.

The original abdominal machine, when used properly, did a good job of isolating the rectus abdominis muscles. The elevating seat removed much of the involvement of the hip flexor muscles. The second abdominal machine, however, by restraining the legs, involved the hip flexors and the abdominals.

The Next Generation abdominal combines the best of the previous abdominal machines. A belt is used to restrain the hips, the upper arms are placed on shoulder-level pads, and a crunch-type shortening of the midsection is performed. The Next Generation abdominal brings into action the rectus abdominis better than previous machines.

The primary function of the rectus abdominis is to bring the rib cage and pelvic girdle closer together. This is also the movement supplied by the Next Generation abdominal machine.

PREEXHAUSTION PRINCIPLE

Q. *On the Nautilus double shoulder machine, should the seat be readjusted after the lateral raise in order to provide a greater range of movement in the overhead press? If so, why?*

A. You should make sure the seat on the double shoulder machine is raised very quickly. A muscle can recover 50 percent of its exhausted strength in about three seconds. For best results, you should move from lateral raise to the overhead press in less than three seconds.

All Nautilus double machines (compound leg, pullover/torso arm, behind neck/torso arm, double chest, and double shoulder) were designed to make use of the preexhaustion principle. The purpose of this principle is to preexhaust a muscle group by performing a single-joint exercise that involves specific muscles. This is immediately followed by a multiple-joint exercise that brings into play other surrounding muscles to force the preexhausted muscles to work even harder.

The primary exercise of the double shoulder machine, the lateral raise, is a single-joint movement that works the deltoids without involving the arms. The secondary exercise, the overhead press, is a multiple-joint movement that involves the deltoids and the arms. When they are done back-to-back the overhead press uses the strength of the triceps to force the preexhausted deltoids to work even harder.

NEGATIVE WORK

Q. *For strength-training purposes, why is negative work more productive than positive work?*

A. A close examination of negative work reveals that it is the most important part not only of strength training but also of a wide variety of other types of training.

First, prestretching, the neurological stimulation required for a high intensity of muscular contraction, comes from negative work. Exercises performed for the purpose of building strength are of very little value without high intensity of work.

Second, negative work reduces your reserve strength better than other methods of training. You can always continue to lower a resistance after you can no longer raise it. This allows you to reach a higher degree of high-intensity work.

Third, full-range exercise designed to work the entire length of a muscle also requires negative work. Negative work provides the back pressure of force that is required in a finishing position of full muscular contraction.

Fourth, stretching is simply impossible without the back pressure provided by negative work. Thus, exercises performed for the purpose of flexibility would be of little use without negative work.

Fifth, negative work makes it possible to exercise a muscle that is too weak to move against even the slightest amount of positive resistance. Thus, negative work is a very valuable tool for the purpose of working muscles that have become weak as a result of injury.

It should be obvious that, if you're concerned about strength, flexibility, or full-range exercise, you should pay close attention to the negative part of all exercises.

REHABILITATION

Q. *How is Nautilus equipment best used in the rehabilitation of an injured athlete?*

A. An injury is usually followed by a rest period of limited activity. Much depends, of course, on the nature of the injury and its severity. As soon as possible following injury diagnosis and correction, the athlete should begin Nautilus training. Naturally, this should be done with the physician's full knowledge.

Uninjured body parts can be exercised in the normal fashion. An athlete with a left-knee injury, for example, can train his complete upper body, right leg, and even the left buttocks. By doing so he can prevent much of the wasting away that would normally occur to both the injured area and the whole body. An individual's level of fitness can even be improved while he is injured.

Excellent results have been obtained by many orthopedic and rehabilitation clinics by using negative-only exercise for rehabilitating an injured area. Initially, an individual recovering from knee surgery will not be able to extend or bend his injured leg against even the lightest resistance. But he can support and lower a limited number of degrees depending on the injury, a minimum of 20 pounds on the leg extension and leg curl machines.

First he lifts the resistance or movement arm with his good leg; then he slowly and smoothly transfers this resistance to his bad leg. The injured leg now supports the movement arm and slowly lowers it to the point of pain. As a safety precaution, the

Rehabilitation of an injured
limb is aided by training the
uninjured body parts in a
high-intensity fashion. This
prevents much of the
atrophy that would normally
occur to the injured limb
and the body. (Photo by
Ellington Darden)

good leg is nearly touching the roller pad at all times. This
raising with the good leg and lowering with the bad leg should
be continued for 8–12 repetitions on both the leg extension
and leg curl machines.

Because of the injured leg's weakness, this procedure
should be repeated twice a day for 14 consecutive days. When
12 lowering repetitions can be performed with the injured leg
the resistance should be increased by 5 percent. No lifting or
positive work should be performed with the injured body part
for the first 2 weeks. The uninjured body parts should be
trained 3 days a week in a normal high-intensity fashion.

After two weeks of daily negative-only exercise for the
injured knee, considerable progress in both strength and
range of movement should be observed. Light positive work

can now be performed with the injured leg. The workouts should be reduced to 2 sets of 8–12 repetitions, 3 times a week, for the injured leg. The first set should be performed by the injured leg in a negative-only style—the movement arm should be lifted with the good leg and lowered with the bad leg. Both the leg extension and the leg curl machines should be operated in this manner. Next, a second set should be performed on each machine in a normal, positive-negative style.

After 2 more weeks of rehabilitation, only one set of 8–12 repetitions of each of the 2 leg exercises should be performed. Other movements for the legs, however, can now be added. Leg presses and calf raises are typical additions.

If proper care is taken, and if the athlete does not become impatient, his injured leg will soon be equal in strength and range of movement to the opposite leg. Usually this signals the athlete's ability to resume his regular skill training or competition. Experience proves that rehabilitation after surgery to knee ligaments usually takes from three to six months. Cartilage removal, chondromalacia, and ligament sprains can be rehabilitated in less time.

The procedures described for the knee can be applied to other injuries, such as those of the ankle, shoulder, elbow, and wrist. But remember that negative-only Nautilus training is the preferred exercise during the first stages of rehabilitation.

For a complete discussion of injuries and rehabilitation, please refer to *The Athlete's Guide to Sports Medicine* (Chicago: Contemporary Books, Inc., 1981).

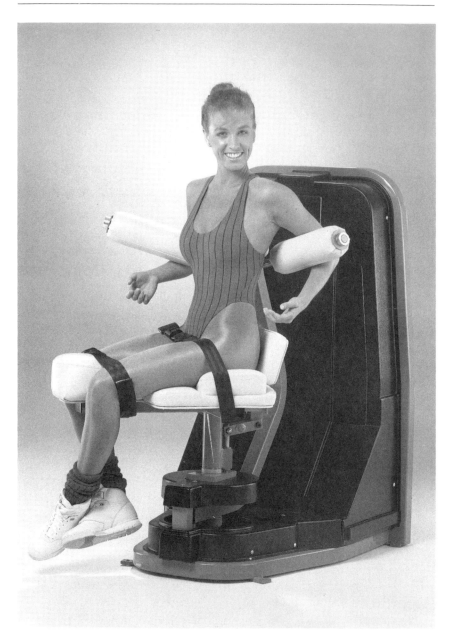

Nautilus builds larger, stronger muscles. Larger, stronger muscles facilitate fat loss because the increased mass burns more calories throughout the day.

25

More Questions
and Answers

LOSING FAT

Q. *How does Nautilus contribute to a fat-loss program?*
A. Nautilus contributes to a fat-loss program in two ways:

First, Nautilus exercise burns calories. The specific number of calories that Nautilus burns depends on the resistance, intensity, and duration used on each exercise.

Second, Nautilus stimulates your muscles to grow larger and stronger. Larger, stronger muscles burn additional calories even at rest, allowing you to lose fat more quickly.

Thus, using Nautilus equipment provides a double reducing effect. Your body requires calories to be burned during Nautilus exercise and additional calories as a result of its produced growth.

THE NAUTILUS DIET

Q. *Do you have a suggested diet to follow for losing fat in conjunction with Nautilus exercise?*

A. Yes, in 1987 I published a book that supplies specific shopping lists, menus, and recipes for losing fat. It is titled *The Nautilus Diet: Ten Weeks to a Brand-New Body* (Boston: Little, Brown, 1987).

The book tells an obese person how to lose fat and build muscle—at the same time. It employs a well-balanced, descending-calorie diet. Men begin with 1,700 calories per day, and women start with 1,400. Men are allowed more calories than women because the average overfat man is larger and has considerably more muscle than does the average overfat woman; thus his body requires more calories.

Every two weeks, until the end of the 10th week, the dietary calories are reduced by 100. Thus, during the 9th and 10th weeks, men are consuming 1,300 calories a day and women are at the 1,000-calorie level. This is as low as the descending-calorie diet ever goes.

Gradually reducing the calories keeps the dieter from developing a ravenous appetite, and it prevents the body from being stressed into its fat preservation stages. In fact, with the descending-calorie diet the opposite will happen. The body will become more efficient at burning fat.

The Nautilus Diet also describes and illustrates an ascending Nautilus exercise program. During the first 2 weeks, both men and women perform only six Nautilus exercises three times per week. Every 2 weeks, until the end of the 10th week, the exercises become harder and more numerous. A maximum of 12 exercises are done during the last 2 weeks.

My experience in working with overweight people for over 20 years has shown me that they respond best to specific guidelines, rather than broad generalities. Thus, *The Nautilus Diet* tells a person exactly what to eat and how to exercise each day for 10 weeks. All an overfat person has to do is to follow the program as directed day by day, week by week, and success is guaranteed.

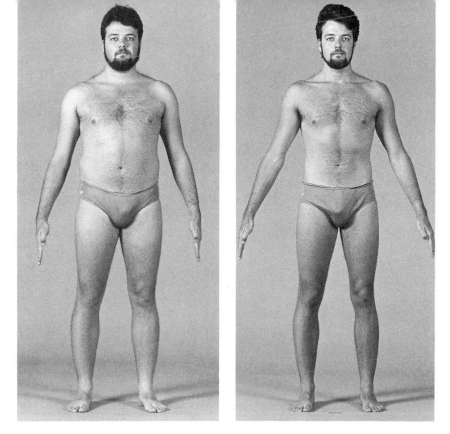

Gary Blandina, 24, went through the 10-week Nautilus Diet program and lost 37¼ pounds of fat. He trimmed his waist by 5¾ inches.

Q. *How much can I expect to lose by following The Nautilus Diet for ten weeks?*

A. The average expectations are as follows:

Men:
- Lose 30 pounds of fat
- Eliminate 4½ inches from your waist
- Build 4 pounds of muscle
- Muscularize your arms and chest

Women:
- Lose 18¾ pounds of fat
- Trim 6⅜ inches off your hips and thighs
- Add 2½ pounds of body-shaping muscle
- Firm your arms and bust

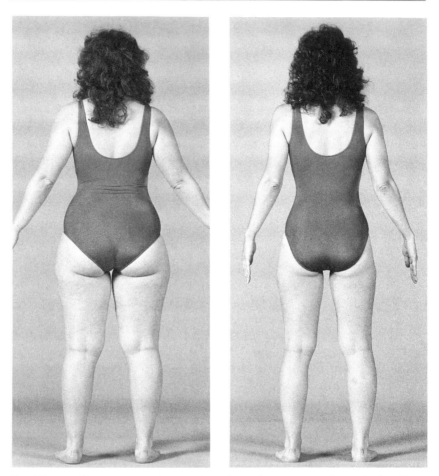

Patti Beran, 30, an art teacher and mother of one, went through the 10-week program twice. She lost 35¼ pounds of fat and reduced her hips by 8⅛ inches and her thighs by 9¼ inches.

The Nautilus Diet is the factual account of a real-life program with real people—as you'll see from the numerous before-and-after photographs of successful participants who have completed the course. If you're interested in losing fat—and keeping it off permanently—The Nautilus Diet is for you!

NAUTILUS AND OTHER ACTIVITIES

Q. What should an individual who likes to combine Nauti-

lus training with sports such as running or racquetball do to get the best results?

A. Under ideal conditions you would run or play racquetball in the morning and Nautilus-train in the afternoon. There should be about a four-hour time lapse between these activities, with a complete day's rest afterward. Thus, you might play racquetball for an hour at 11:00 A.M., eat a light lunch at 12:30 P.M., and train on Nautilus machines around 4:00 or 5:00 P.M. The following day you would rest, relax, and recover. An every-other-day schedule produces the best combined results.

Most people, however, because of the inconvenience of training twice in one day, would rather run or play racquetball on one day and use Nautilus on the next. Or they will try to do both activities on the same day with only a brief rest in between. Neither of these methods has proved to be superior in results to the first method discussed.

DEVELOPING QUICKNESS

Q. Can training on Nautilus equipment improve an athlete's quickness?

A. Quickness is a product of many factors, including (1) the amount of muscle on the body, (2) the amount of fat, (3) the muscle-mass-to-body-weight ratio, (4) skill, (5) bodily proportions, and (6) motivation.

The easiest way to accelerate quickness is to increase your muscle mass, which will favorably change your ratio of muscle mass to body weight. The most effective way to accomplish this is through Nautilus training combined with a well-balanced diet.

BODYBUILDING AND NAUTILUS

Q. I'm interested in bodybuilding. What's the best routine for me to follow?

A. Nautilus routines for bodybuilding have been discussed thoroughly in *The Nautilus Bodybuilding Book* (Chicago: Contemporary Books, Inc., 1989) and *The Nautilus Advanced*

Bodybuilding Book (New York: Simon & Schuster, 1984). Both these books apply to the use of Nautilus equipment.

Two other books, *High-Intensity Bodybuilding* (New York: Putnam, 1984) and *Super High-Intensity Bodybuilding* (New York: Putnam, 1986), detail how Nautilus training principles are used with free weights. A third book, *Massive Muscles in 10 Weeks* (New York: Putnam, 1987), describes the use of the new Nautilus leverage machines for bodybuilding.

In 10 weeks Eddie Mueller added 18 pounds of solid muscle to his body by training intensely on the Nautilus leverage equipment. He also gained 2 inches on his arms, 4 inches on his chest, and 4½ inches on his thighs.

NAUTILUS LEVERAGE MACHINES

Q. *What are the Nautilus leverage machines?*

A. The Nautilus leverage machines do not employ cams to vary the resistance. They vary the resistance by controlling the leverage factors. Futhermore, they do not have self-contained weight stacks. Olympic-style barbell plates must be added to the movement arms to supply the resistance.

Because of the design simplicity of the leverage machines and the lack of selectorized weight stacks, the price is much lower than that of standard Nautilus machines. Nautilus leverage machines, therefore, are especially attractive to facilities that already have barbell equipment, such as high schools, colleges, athletic teams, and bodybuilding gyms.

In 1988, Nautilus is manufacturing the following leverage machines:

- Leverage High and Back
- Leverage Leg Press
- Leverage Leg Extension
- Leverage Leg Curl
- Leverage Pullover
- Leverage Bench Press
- Leverage Seated Dip
- Leverage Lateral Raise
- Leverage 10° Chest
- Leverage Chest/Back (Features incline press and torso arm pulldown)
- Leverage Rowing Plus (Features rowing and shoulder shrug)
- Leverage Biceps/Triceps
- Leverage Chin/Dip
- Leverage Gripper
- Leverage 4-Way Neck

Basic instructions for the leverage machines are the same as for comparable selectorized machines. Two examples, the leverage hip and back and the leverage leg extension, are shown on the following pages.

Leverage Hip and Back

1. Enter machine from either side.
2. Lie on back and place legs over top of padded movement arm.
3. Slide forward until hip joints are aligned with axes of movement arm.
4. Fasten seat belt snugly across pelvic girdle (not across midsection).
5. Grasp handles lightly.
6. Extend hips smoothly by thrusting both thighs slowly forward and down. Keep knees together.
7. Pause in extended position, arch lower back, and contract buttocks. Legs should be straight and toes pointed.
8. Bend hips and allow knees to move slowly toward chest.
9. Repeat.

Leverage Leg Extension

1. Sit in machine.
2. Place feet behind roller pads.
3. Fasten seat belt across hips.
4. Keep head and shoulders against seat back.
5. Grasp handles lightly.
6. Straighten legs smoothly.
7. Pause in top position.
8. Lower slowly to bottom.
9. Repeat.

NAUTILUS HOME MACHINES

Q. I see that Nautilus is now manufacturing machines for home use. How do the home machines compare with the standard commercial Nautilus machines?

A. In 1987 Nautilus introduced four dual-function machines and one single-function machine to the home market. The primary differences between the home machines and the commercial machines are as follows:

- Home machines are lighter in design than the commercial machines. Home machines are not manufactured for commercial, heavy-duty use. They are built for the home.
- Home machines have dual functions, while most commercial machines are limited to one movement.
- Home machines do not have selectorized weight stacks. Weight plates must be added to the central column of each unit.
- Home machines and commercial machines are both equipped with Nautilus cams to vary the resistance correctly.
- Home machines give you a full-body workout in a 12-foot-by 12-foot area of your den, living room, basement, or garage.
- Home machines are much less expensive than commercial machines. The average home machine sells for $500–600.

The Nautilus training principles that were described in Chapter 7 apply to the home machines. Specific directions on the use of each machine follow on the next few pages.

Home Leg Machine, Leg Extension

1. Adjust movement arm to lower position and secure lock pin.
2. Sit on seat.
3. Place ankles behind roller pads.
4. Fasten seat belt across hips.
5. Straighten both legs smoothly.
6. Pause in top position.
7. Lower slowly.
8. Repeat.

Home Leg Machine, Leg Curl

1. Adjust movement arm to upper position and secure lock pin.
2. Sit on seat.
3. Place ankles in front of lower pads and knees behind upper pads. Be careful and avoid twisting knees.
4. Push bony area below kneecaps into upper roller pad while pulling lower leg against lower pad.
5. Bend legs smoothly.
6. Pause in contracted position.
7. Lower weight slowly.
8. Repeat.

Home Chest/Shoulder Machine, Chest

1. Position bench for chest exercise by securing wheels in track.
2. Raise movement arms to upper position and secure lock pin.
3. Sit on bench and lie on back with head at higher end.
4. Position elbows and forearms behind movement arms.
5. Rotate elbows up and across torso.
6. Pause in contracted position.
7. Lower weight slowly.
8. Repeat.

Home Chest/Shoulder Machine, Shoulder

1. Grasp handle at end of bench and roll bench away from machine.
2. Adjust each movement arm to lower positions and secure lock pin.
3. Sit on bench with back against machine, feet on floor, and knees slightly bent.
4. Place upper arms by sides and bend elbows to 90 degrees. Contact should be made with movement arms.
5. Raise elbows smoothly to chin level.
6. Pause.
7. Lower elbows slowly.
8. Repeat.

Home Arm Machine, Biceps

1. Flip up handles on movement arm.
2. Rotate movement arm to lower position and secure lock pin.
3. Straddle seat and grasp handles. Place elbows on padded elbow rest. Bend elbows to 90 degrees.
4. Sit, keeping elbows bent. As you sit, movement arm will rise.
5. Keep shoulders down and wrists straight. Allow machine to straighten elbows.
6. Bend elbows smoothly as far as possible.
7. Pause in contracted position.
8. Lower weight slowly.
9. Repeat.

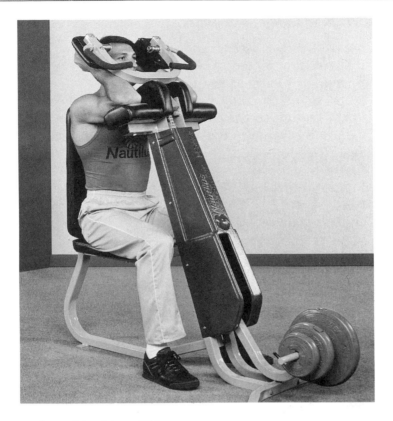

Home Arm Machine, Triceps
1. Move handgrips out of way by folding them under movement arm.
2. Raise movement arm to upper position and secure lock pin.
3. Push and hold movement arm forward. Straddle seat. Sit, placing elbows on elbow rests. Keep elbows level or slightly higher than shoulders.
4. Place hands on movement arm with palms facing each other.
5. Straighten both arms smoothly.
6. Pause.
7. Bend elbows and lower weight slowly.
8. Repeat.

Home Waist Machine, Abdominal

1. Make sure seat faces front of machine and weight arm.
2. Pull selector pin to outer position and leave there to engage proper gear for this exercise.
3. Sit on seat facing machine.
4. Position shins so they are just contacting shin pads.
5. Adjust movement arm pads to comfortable position against chest.
6. Interlace hands across navel.
7. Bend forward smoothly at waist.
8. Pause.
9. Lower weight slowly.
10. Repeat.

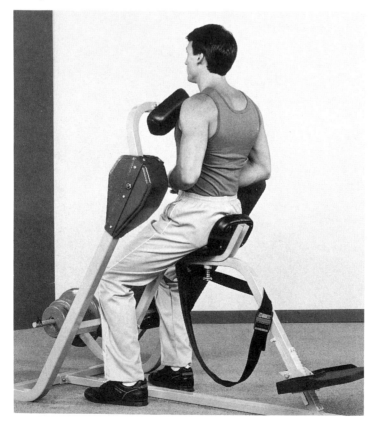

Home Waist Machine, Lower Back

1. Pull seat straight up so it faces rear of machine. Allow seat to lock down.
2. Push in pin lock on movement arm to engage proper gear for lower back exercise.
3. Sit on seat facing away from weight arm.
4. Place feet on footrest, adjusting it to allow a 45-degree bend in your knees.
5. Adjust movement arm pads to comfortable position on upper back.
6. Strap belt across upper thighs.
7. Interlace hands across navel.
8. Lean back smoothly against movement arm. Keep head and neck stable. Keep constant tension on belt by push-ing up with legs, as if trying to stand.

9. Pause in extended position.
10. Lower weight slowly.
11. Repeat.

Home Rotary Torso Machine

1. Sit on one side of seat, straddling the middle.
2. Reach back and hook a roller pad in the crook of each elbow.
3. Tighten elbows around pads so they are close to back. Place hands palms up with their inside edge against waist.

4. Position feet on floor, gently squeezing saddle between knees to stabilize lower body.
5. Twist torso smoothly into resistance. Do not move hands.
6. Pause in contracted position.
7. Lower weight slowly.
8. Repeat.
9. Straddle seat on opposite side of machine and work with other side.

Q. *Does Nautilus plan on introducing more new equipment?*

A. Yes. Currently, Nautilus has other machines available for the home:

• A multi-station machine for the lower body and a multi-station machine for the upper body. Each of these machines has six or seven stations with separate cams and weight stacks.

- A line of stationary bicycles.
- A high-quality line of free-weight benches and racks.
- More specialized diet and exercise programs, which
  will be similar to *The Nautilus Diet*. For example, *Big
  Arms in Six Weeks*, *The Six-Week Muscle-Fat Make-
  over* (a diet and exercise program for women only),
  and *32 Days to a 32-Inch Waist*.

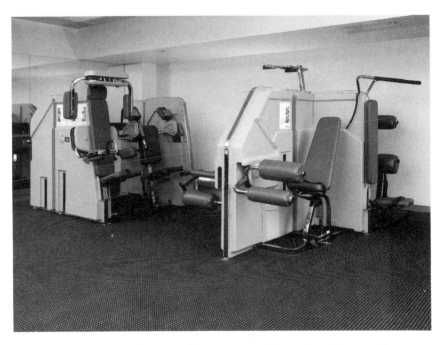

The multi-station machine combines 11 Nautilus stations into two frames
that can be placed into a room as small as 16 feet by 26 feet, or an area of
416 square feet. The stations on the right frame are leg curl, leg extension,
multi-exercise, abdominal, lower back, and torso arm. On the left frame
in the photo, the stations are pullover, lateral raise, chest/arm cross,
triceps, and biceps.

NEW NAUTILUS RESEARCH ON REPETITIONS

Q. *I've read literature from Nautilus written by Arthur Jones, which discusses some recent physiological discoveries from testing people on your computerized machines. Will these new findings have any effect on my future Nautilus training?*

A. Most of the discoveries made using the Nautilus computerized machines apply primarily to rehabilitation, sportsmedicine, and research testing. One finding, however, may have a profound effect on a few people who train on Nautilus. This finding concerns the number of repetitions certain trainees should do in their Nautilus exercise for best results. Before discussing repetitions, let's briefly examine the new computerized machines—what they are and how they are used.

Five highly sophisticated models of traditional Nautilus exercise equipment have been outfitted with computer technology, forming the Nautilus Medical Machine System. More machines may well join the Medical Machine line at a later time, but currently the computerized units are the leg extension, leg curl, abdominal, rotary torso, and back extension.

In testing several hundred subjects, we've found that not every Nautilus trainee responds optimally to 8–12 repetitions. Approximately 70 percent do, but 30 percent do not. Some trainees require higher repetitions. Other trainees need lower repetitions.

The bottom line, obviously, is that you make progress on each Nautilus exercise you perform. You get stronger. How much stronger? Approximately 5 percent every two weeks on each basic Nautilus exercise.

Arthur Jones now feels that a key factor in muscular growth stimulation is inroad. Inroad is the depletion of momentary strength from a set of an exercise. If you make too little of an inroad, then your muscles are not stimulated enough to grow. If you make too much of an inroad, then your muscles may be stimulated but unable to grow effectively because the stimulation has been too deep. Jones believes that the proper inroad, the inroad that stimulates the most efficient muscular growth, is approximately 20 percent for all your major muscles. In other words, the number of repetitions that you perform should reduce your starting level of strength by 20 percent.

Thus, when you perform repetitions with 80 percent of your maximum and fail from lack of strength, you fail because you have reduced your starting level of strength by slightly more than 20 percent. You have made an inroad of slightly more than 20 percent—and this is good.

Taking the number of repetitions that you do with 80 percent of your maximum and dividing this number into 20 gives you the amount of inroad made per repetition. Research shows that most people make about 2 percent inroad per repetition and fail at 10–12 repetitions. People who can involve more muscle fibers make a greater inroad per repetition and fail sooner. In fact, we've tested several people who could only do 2–3 repetitions before they failed. On the other hand, we've tested several people who made less than 0.5 percent inroad per repetition and could do 20–30 repetitions before they had to stop.

Obviously, there are not many people who fail at the extremes of 2 repetitions and 30 repetitions. But they do exist. And they need to be trained accordingly.

If you are making at least a 5 percent improvement every two weeks, then do not modify your program. Continue to train using the 8-to-12-repetition plan. You are making the correct inroad into your starting level of strength and recovery ability.

On the other hand, if your progress is not up to par, then you may require either higher or lower repetitions than the traditional 8–12. Since most people do not have access to the new Nautilus testing machines, here are 10 steps to follow using two standard Nautilus machines to evaluate your repetition inroad.

1. Use the leg extension to test your lower body and the pullover to test your upper body. Complete the entire test for the leg extension before doing the pullover.

2. Determine the greatest amount of weight you can perform one time in proper form. This becomes your one-repetition maximum and should be done in this manner:
   (a) Warm up by doing 6 repetitions with a light weight on the machine.
   (b) Continue your warm-up by doing 3 repetitions with a resistance you would normally do for 10 repetitions.
   (c) Add 10–15 percent more resistance to the machine and try for one repetition.
   (d) Rest two minutes and try 5 percent more for one repetition.
   (e) Rest another two minutes and try 2.5–5 percent more. Do not cheat. Do not jerk the resistance. Keep the movements smooth.
   (f) Rest and continue adding a small amount of resistance to the machine until you can no longer complete a full-range repetition.
   (g) Record your one-repetition maximum, which is the highest weight in pounds that you performed correctly throughout a full range of movement.
3. Rest at least five minutes.
4. Take 80 percent of your one-repetition maximum and perform as many repetitions as possible in proper form. Keep the repetitions strict. Do not cheat.
5. Make a written note of the number of repetitions.
6. Multiply the number of repetitions by .15.
7. Round off the resulting figure to the nearest whole number.
8. Add this whole number to your 80 percent repetitions. This becomes the high end of your repetition guideline.
9. Subtract the same whole number from your 80 percent repetitions. This becomes the low end of your repetition guideline.
10. Apply your leg extension guideline to all your lower body exercises. Do the same thing with your upper body exercises by using your guideline for the pullover.

Conclusion

Nautilus training, understood and applied properly, makes you stronger, leaner, more flexible, more enduring, and less prone to injury. With Nautilus, it does not take years to produce dramatic results. Improvement can be seen within weeks and is obvious within a few months.

Yes, Nautilus, the symbol of geometric perfection, was reborn in the form of machines that are now revolutionizing physical fitness.

Join the Nautilus revolution today!

A Nautilus-trained body is strong, lean, and shapely.

Bibliography

Darden, Ellington. *New High-Intensity Bodybuilding*. New York: Putnam Publishing Group, 1990.

———. *The Nautilus Diet: Ten Weeks to a Brand-New Body*. Boston: Little, Brown, 1987.

———. *The Nautilus Woman, Revised Edition*. New York: Simon and Schuster, 1986.

———. *The Nautilus Bodybuilding Book, Revised Edition*. Chicago: Contemporary Books, 1989.

———. *The Nautilus Nutrition Book*. Chicago: Contemporary Books, 1981.

———. *The Athlete's Guide to Sports Medicine*. Chicago: Contemporary Books, 1981.

———. "Which 'Iso' Builds Strength—Isometric? Isotonic? Isokinetic?" *National Racquetball* 9: 40–43, March 1980.

———. "What Research Says about Positive and Negative Work." *Scholastic Coach* 45: 6, 7, October 1975.

Deutsch, Ronald M. *The New Nuts among the Berries*. Palo Alto, California: Bull Publishing Co., 1977.

Fox, Edward L., and Mathews, Donald K. *The Physiological Basis of Physical Education and Athletics* (Third Edition). Philadelphia: Saunders College Publishing, 1981.

Goldberg, Alfred L., and others. "Mechanisms of Work-Induced Hypertrophy of Skeletal Muscle." *Medicine and Science in Sports* 7: 248–61, 1975.

Hutchins, Ken. *The Ultimate Exercise Protocol: Super Slow*. Casselberry, Florida: Media Support, 1989.

Jobl, Ernst. "Physique and Performance." *American Corrective Therapy Journal* 27: 99–114, 1973.

Jones, Arthur. "The Upper-Body Squat." *Iron Man* 29, 5: 41, 47, 71, June 1970.

———. *Nautilus Training Principles, Bulletin No. 1*. DeLand, Florida: Nautilus Sports/Medical Industries, 1970.

———. *Nautilus Training Principles, Bulletin No. 2*. DeLand, Florida: Nautilus Sports/Medical Industries, 1971.

———. "High-Intensity Strength Training." *Scholastic Coach* 42: 46, 47, 117, 118, May 1973.

Kirshenbaum, Jerry, and Sullivan Robert. "Hold on There, America." *Sports Illustrated* 58: 60–70, February 7, 1983

Komi, P. V., and Buskirk, E. R. "Effects of Eccentric and Concentric Muscle Conditioning on Tension and Electrical Activity of Human Muscle." *Ergonomics* 15: 417–34, 1972.

MacDonald, Simon G. G., and Burns, Desmond M. *Physics for the Life and Health Sciences*. Reading, Massachusetts: Addison-Wesley, 1975.

Michener, James A. *Sports in America*. New York: Random House, 1976.

Rasch, Philip J., and Burke, Roger K. *Kinesiology and Applied Anatomy*. Philadelphia: Lea and Febiger, 1978.

Sheldon, William. *Atlas of Men*. New York: Harper and Brothers, 1954.

Singer, Robert N. *The Learning of Motor Skills*. New York: Macmillan, 1982.

Westcott, Wayne L. *Strength Fitness, Expanded Second Edition*. Boston: Allyn and Bacon, 1987.

Index